ESPIONAGE
DOWN & DIRTY

ESPIONAGE
DOWN & DIRTY

Tony Lesce

Loompanics Unlimited
Port Townsend, Washington

This book is sold for informational purposes only. The publisher will not be held accountable for the use or misuse of the information contained in this book.

ESPIONAGE: DOWN AND DIRTY
© 1991 by Tony Lesce
Printed in USA

Published by:
Loompanics Unlimited
PO Box 1197
Port Townsend, WA 98368

Loompanics Unlimited is a division of Loompanics Enterprises, Inc.

Cover by Kevin Martin

ISBN 1-55950-068-9
Library of Congress
  Catalog Card Number 91-060972

CONTENTS

Introduction

〰〰〰〰〰〰〰〰〰〰〰〰〰〰〰〰〰〰〰〰〰〰〰〰〰〰〰〰

Espionage is both glamorous and sordid. The glamour comes from the treatment given in both the documentary and fictional media. Jingoistic propaganda glorifies the CIA, just as in other countries it glamorizes their espionage services. Rudyard Kipling called espionage the "Great Game," in his novel, *Kim*. Other fiction writers play up espionage as a glorious adventure. The sordid aspect comes from the way the "game" is actually played.

Betrayal is the name of the game. A traitor betrays his country. The spy takes advantage of contacts he makes within the target country, and betrays friendships. The spymaster may betray one or more of his agents, including an entire network, to serve what he considers a higher purpose.

In the half-light of espionage, hardly anything is as it seems. There are secrets, false identities and documents, cover stories, lies and evasions, denials, and a pervasive atmosphere of conspiracy. This atmosphere is attractive to some people, but it's also very dangerous.

If you're running the spy desk at an embassy, you soon find out that your bosses at headquarters tell you only what they want you to know. The ambassador, your nominal superior, as a rule knows even less than you. You also find out that defectors and walk-in sources are not always what they seem. Secret documents a walk-in hands you may be partial fabrications, with enough truth to make them appear valid. A walk-in may be a "provocation," sent to lead you into a trap. A fake defector, sent to plant "disinformation" with you, may betray real agents to establish credibility. At times, entire secret operations are part of a "disinformation" effort, to mislead you and cause you to waste time and resources following false leads.

Espionage ethics are practically non-existent. Expediency is the prime rule. This is very obvious when espionage organizations get into sabotage, which often injures and kills innocent people. A spymaster who orders a sabotage operation allows nobody to be neutral. Anyone in the vicinity of the target is in danger of being caught in the cross-fire.

This is the same mentality that leaders of terrorist organizations adopt. George Habash, leader of the

Popular Front for the Liberation of Palestine, (PFLP) stated it this way:

"In today's world, no one is innocent, no one a neutral. A man is either with the oppressed or he is with the oppressors."

Another way of denying anyone the right to be neutral is:

"If you're not part of the solution, you're part of the problem."

The simplest way to express it is:

"You're either for us or against us."

This sophistry is the spy's way of justifying injury to innocent persons. Anyone who isn't actively helping him is, in his view, an active or potential enemy. To the spy or spymaster, the entire world is either helping or hindering him, which justifies any action to attain his goals.

1

Espionage Goals

~~~~~~

We have to note that most of the useful information governments seek about each other is not secret. Information from open sources makes up the bulk of the data because it's not practical to try to classify it. Street maps, railroad timetables, identities of government leaders and employees, and other information are impossible to conceal without building high walls around everything in the country. However, in some of the Eastern Bloc countries, street maps and telephone directories have for years been classified information. This policy has relaxed only recently.

Espionage is only one part of a government's information-gathering effort. The entire field is usually called "intelligence," a high-blown term that suggests that its practitioners are particularly bright people. In reality, some are, and others aren't. Some of those who seem very bright make appalling mistakes. Some of the stupid ones hang on to their jobs only because heavy secrecy prevents their civilian overseers from knowing the true extent of their failures. If you're working in an "intelligence" organization, you might be dismayed by the stupidity of some of your bosses and fellow employees, until you decide to go along and become part of the "system."

Openly Available Information

Intelligence, or information, comes from several types of sources. Much comes from open sources, such as scanning another country's newspapers, and monitoring its radio and TV programs. If you work for an intelligence service, the odds are that you occupy a desk, and scrutinize newspapers and magazines, trying to put together a picture of what's really happening in the country you're studying.

A good source of information is the observations of diplomats, who often can travel as much as they wish in the host country. Few countries limit the travels of foreign diplomats. If you're serving under the cover of a diplomatic post, you'll be able to roam at will, seeing what the country's citizens see, unless you're in a country with severe restrictions on diplomats' travel.

Yet another source is interviewing returned travelers. Business contacts also provide information, because many companies have offices in foreign countries, and obtaining information from these helps round out the picture. News organizations often do informal information gathering for the mother country, and reporters are accredited to practically every government in the world. Governments regularly debrief their journalists who have returned from abroad, and even try to obtain information from sympathetic foreign and neutral journalists. In some cases, students who spend several years studying in another country are good sources of information. In some outstanding cases, an advanced student can bring back high-tech information the host country doesn't think is important enough to restrict. Peter Kapitza, known in Russia as the "father" of their nuclear bomb, spent the early years of his career studying nuclear physics in England. As a graduate student, he was on the cutting edge of nuclear technology, and when he returned to Russia he took his knowledge with him.

Intelligence functionaries who pore over the target country's newspapers, analyze its radio and TV programs, and interview travelers to tease out bits of information possibly useful to their employers, are the bean-counters of the intelligence world. They're the ones with the nine-to-five jobs and homes in the suburbs. As with other office workers, their careers are desperately dull. If this is your job, look at the bright side — you could do worse working for an insurance company, and earn less.

Secret
Information

Most governments try to keep secret only critical information, such as their codes and ciphers, military and diplomatic plans, intentions, and technical details of new weapon systems. They also make serious efforts to obtain information about other governments' top secret codes, plans, and weapons.

Much information about weapon systems is available with little effort, because the weapons are often on public display. A patriotic parade, with equipment rolling by and aircraft overflying it, shows anyone attending what the weapons are. Some technical details aren't open to view, but obtaining these is often easier than it seems. Captured weapons, such as Soviet tanks disabled and rounded up by the Israelis during the Lebanon invasion of 1982, provided a close view of existing Soviet armored vehicle technology. At times, salesmen employed by a defense plant will give away information on weapons built in his factory at trade shows. Most diplomatic information is available through the news media, the diplomatic gossip circuit, or by inference from a country's actions.

There are two crucial categories of information which governments try to keep deeply buried, at the same time trying to uncover them from other governments. These are codes and ciphers, and intelligence agencies and their activities. Because this information is top-secret, intelligence agencies resort to espionage to obtain it.

"Cryptosystems," the general term for all types of codes and ciphers, are crucial because they protect the government's communications. Anyone who can read your crypto traffic can obtain your other secrets, too. If you can steal or break another power's cryptosystems, you will eventually uncover all of their secrets, as well. This is why the Walker spy ring did so well selling crypto secrets to the Russians. John Walker earned a lot of money, some of which he rat-holed, and the government hasn't recovered all of it.

Intelligence agencies are also extremely important, because they deal in obtaining information about other powers, and protecting domestic secret information. If you can find out what your rival's foreign intelligence agency is doing, you'll know how successful they've been in penetrating your secrets, and whether they have any agents within your government or defense industries. If you know what their counterintelligence service is doing, you'll know how successful they've been in combating your penetration efforts against them, and whether they're feeding you false information through captured agents.

Wartime espionage is somewhat different. Governments close their frontiers, and censor the media, closing channels of communication. Information that normally is freely available becomes top-secret. The enemy espionage agency tries to set up a network of watchers, to observe and report troop movements, train schedules, and the activities in seaports and airports.

Sabotage

Espionage often overlaps with sabotage and other clandestine activities. Although purists in the field try to keep them separate, because they feel that sabotage violates the low profile necessary for successful espionage, they often are overruled for expediency. If you're a spy in the field, and your control orders you to carry out sabotage, you can expect a short career, because sabotage requires you to stick your neck out a mile.

During the 1940s, for example, the Soviet Intelligence Services (there are two) operated five spy rings inside Sweden, one of their western neighbors. Among the agents were saboteurs, probably including some "sleepers," armed with explosives, with the mission of disrupting communication and transportation in case of war.[1] As we'll see, the Israelis mixed espionage and sabotage in Egypt, and counter-spies uncovered a Soviet plan to sabotage British defenses in case of war with the NATO powers.

During the 1950s and 1960s the Egyptian government tried very hard to develop advanced weapons, such as guided rockets. They recruited some German scientists to help them. Israeli agents, alarmed by this, began a campaign to drive these German scientists out of Egypt. They began sending letter-bombs to German scientists working in Egypt. They reinforced this by sending threatening letters, mentioning that these scientists should leave Egypt if they cared for their safety and the safety of their wives and children.[2]

The campaign went beyond Egypt, and took in more than the scientists themselves. Heinz Krug, manager of the Munich office of a company supplying rocket parts, disappeared, and his abandoned car was found a few days later. Another German connected with the program became the victim of an assassination attempt while driving along a narrow road in Germany. There are also several forms of serious harassment. The secretary of one of the Germans employed in Egypt opened a letter addressed to him. The letter exploded causing her serious injury and blindness. Five subordinates of an Egyptian general connected with the rocket program died when a bomb addressed to their chief exploded.[3]

Closely allied to sabotage is assassination. Many of the world's secret services have assassination sections, and there's no way of telling exactly how many people they dispose of discreetly. Occasionally, a mistake comes to light. An Israeli hit team, gunning for Arabs in reprisal for the killing of some of their athletes at Munich in 1973, shot down the wrong man in Lillehammer, Norway, mistaking him for an Arab terrorist named Ali Hassan Salameh. David Arbel, Sylvia Rafael and Abraham Gehmer, three of the agents involved in the mistaken shooting of a Moroccan waiter, did not escape, and spent time in a Norwegian prison.[4]

At times, innocent people die by design. The Pan American airliner destroyed by an explosion over Lockerbie, Scotland, in 1988 was one example. The picture of exactly what happened has become more muddy since the allegation that the explosion was linked to an operation by the American Drug Enforcement Administration. An attempt that failed was the smuggling of a bomb into an El-Al jumbo jet in London, in 1986. A Jordanian named Nezar Hindiwi gave a parcel to his pregnant Irish girlfriend to take with her on board the airliner. She didn't know the contents of the parcel, nor that her boyfriend considered her to be the expendable delivery system.[5] In this case, Hindiwi may have been trying to cope with an annoying personal problem while discharging his duties to his group, hoping to take care of both at once.

Espionage Organizations

Most espionage organizations follow a certain pattern, because it allows efficient operation. First, there's a spy headquarters or directorate in the home country. This is where the top executives work, taking orders from the country's political leaders, recruiting agents for foreign duty, and administering the entire effort. This is also where training takes place for those slated for both domestic and foreign assignments.

Another headquarters function is research into many topics, such as foreign nations' objectives and policies, and biographies of world leaders and their staffs. Much of this information is publicly available, and the main task is to assemble it in a form convenient to read or run a briefing. The esoteric research is the fun part of an espionage agency. This is where laboratory workers dream up the James Bond gadgets, and other exotic toys.

Mind control, using drugs, electric shocks, and other techniques, has been a high-priority research topic among various espionage agencies for years. During World War II, experimenters at Dachau, a concentration camp near Munich, Germany, conducted tests to determine the effects of mescaline upon human beings. Test subjects were camp inmates, not volunteers, and experimenters spiked their food and drink with the drug. The purpose was to find a "truth drug," to serve as an interrogation aid. The American O.S.S. also experimented with drugs for enhancing subjects' replies. One was marijuana, which O.S.S. agents administered in the subjects' cigarettes. Unknowing subjects included a New York gangster and several American servicemen.[6]

After the war, the CIA took up the task, using drugs on unwilling subjects to test their value for mind control, hypnotism, causing memory loss, and other forms of psychological manipulation. Part of this experimentation was on unknowing subjects, some of whom were confined in psychiatric hospitals. These patients were injected with substances for testing, and some of the doctors cooperating in the experiments did not even know what it was they were injecting. There were at least two deaths resulting from these experiments. A New York tennis pro named Harold Blauer died one morning while being subjected to a drug study, but for years his family did not know the exact circumstances of his death.[7]

Another part of the drug testing program was to set up "safe houses" as bases and testing centers. CIA agents employed prostitutes to lure ordinary citizens to them, where they were subjected to various drugs administered in a covert manner. One example was a swizzle stick coated with a drug. Another was an aerosol can to spray LSD into the air during a party.[8]

Some of the most outlandish experiments took place outside our borders. A Canadian psychiatrist named Cameron undertook to test massive doses of both drugs and electroshock treatments as methods of "deprogramming" test subjects. The purpose was to destroy the personality and rebuild it to new specifications, so as to create new behavior patterns. With a combination of barbiturates, tranquilizers, and shock treatments, Cameron caused his patients to become confused and disoriented, the first step in creating a blank slate for reprogramming. The results were disappointing, as the human personality is not quite as cut-and-dried as Cameron had expected.[9]

The politics of running an espionage organization can be very convoluted. It's necessary to convince your political bosses that your function is vital to the survival of the country, to obtain larger budgets and more power for your agency. A good way to do this is by regularly delivering alarming estimates of enemy capabilities and intentions, playing the same game that the leaders of the armed forces do at budget time. The other side of the coin is using secrecy to conceal your blunders, as did the CIA when their drug experiments killed Harold Blauer.

If your information is inadequate, incomplete, or false, you simply bluff it through. Your political bosses won't know until it's too late, giving you a lot of time to think up excuses, or even to retire. An example of this is the CIA's erroneous intelligence regarding Vietnam. The CIA had not developed good sources on the communist side, partly because of Vietcong counter-intelligence operations. Instead, the CIA scooped up second-hand information from the South Vietnamese, who were inept, corrupt, and heavily infiltrated by VC. This erroneous information led to a totally false picture built up by the planners in Washington. A further problem was that, during the Vietnam War era, information from the CIA did not really count unless it confirmed the preconceived notions of the top civilian and military planners.[10]

In foreign countries, there must be an espionage base, and a network of agents. The head spy in a foreign country is the "resident." He may actually reside in that country under diplomatic cover, or be totally illegal. He may have a false identity, as did Soviet Russia's Colonel Abel, or he may even be in a neighboring country. For years, the People's Republic of China maintained a residency in Toronto, Canada, for espionage against the United States, because China did not have diplomatic relations with the U.S. Larry Wu-Tai Chin, a Chinese infiltrator in the CIA, regularly passed his information to the Chinese resident in Toronto.[11]

The resident operates a network, including talent spotters, recruiters, control agents, couriers, and others. The more numerous and affluent spy agencies can afford a large staff, but small countries' spies have to do almost everything themselves. Much of the actual work is dull and tedious, unlike what we see in fiction.

Sources

1. *The FBI-KGB War*, Robert J. Lamphere, NY, Berkeley Books, 1987, p. 24.

2. *The Mossad*, Dennis Eisenberg, Uri Dan, and Eli Landau, NY, Paddington Press, 1978, p. 143.

3. *Ibid.*, p. 183.

4. *Spyclopedia*, Richard Deacon, NY, Silver Arrow Books, 1988, p. 362. Also see: *By Way of Deception*, Victor Ostrovsky, NY, St. Martin's Press, 1990, pp. 205-206. According to this account, by a former Mossad officer, Salameh set up the Israeli team by feeding them false information.

   The Israelis have an assassination section in their secret service, known as "Kidon," or bayonet. These are three 12-man teams whose only function is to liquidate those whom their masters wish dead. See *By Way of Deception*, pp. 117-118.

5. *Ibid.*, p. 379.

6. *The Search for the Manchurian Candidate*, John Marks, NY, Dell, 1988, pp. 5-8.

7. *Ibid.*, pp. 70-93.

8. *Ibid.*, pp. 94-112.

9. *Ibid.*, pp. 139-166.

10. *Spying For America*, Nathan Miller, NY, Dell Books, 1989, pp. 432-433.

11. *Merchants of Treason*, Thomas B. Allen and Norman Polmar, NY, Dell Books, 1988, p. 379.

2

The Spy
In Fiction

〰〰〰〰〰〰〰〰〰〰〰〰〰〰〰〰〰〰〰〰〰〰〰〰〰〰〰〰〰〰〰〰〰〰

Spy fiction has become a genre in literature, and there has been a rash of both books and motion pictures dealing with spies. Apart from very few semi-documentaries, most are pure fiction, and the most successful ones present a highly romanticized picture of the spy's world.

John Buchan, the British author who wrote *The 39 Steps*, was an outdoors type who reveled in chase stories. *The 39 Steps* is a chase story, about a German master spy who infiltrates the British Government by his ability to disguise himself as almost anyone. The story's hero encounters a beautiful woman who is menaced by the spy ring, and they take off on a chase around the British Isles, pursued by enemy agents until the final confrontation.

Probably the first writer of spy fiction in this century who did not hopelessly romanticize and distort the world of espionage was Somerset Maugham, a British author who served in the Secret Intelligence Service during World War I. He spent most of his time in Switzerland, observing the moves of the rival German Intelligence Service, and his novel, *Ashenden*, is a semi-documentary based on his experiences. The plot is unimportant, as the novel is episodic and disjointed, but the atmosphere of espionage comes across to the reader very well. The admonition of the colonel who gives the hero his assignment is unforgettable:

"If you do well, you'll get no thanks; if you get in trouble, you'll get no help."

This reflects the cynicism that pervades the British espionage establishment, and others as well. We'll see examples of how cynically spymasters view their agents in later chapters. Loyalty flows only one way, upward, and if the agent is caught, his masters will not only abandon him, but deny that they ever knew him. *Ashenden* is a gloomy story, and did not enjoy the overwhelming success of more upbeat fiction, such as the James Bond stories. It did, however, make it into film during the 1930s, as one of Alfred Hitchcock's early thrillers.

The best-known fictional spy during the second half of the 20th century was Ian Fleming's James Bond. All of Fleming's James Bond novels followed the winning formula of fast cars, sex, and violence. The character of James Bond was a fairly attractive man with a variety of skills, including martial arts, firearms marksmanship, and sex. Bond always won in the end, destroying an arch-enemy of civilization despite various attempts to kill and torture him. The Bond novels were outstanding commercial successes, although they departed from reality in many significant ways.

Bond, with his fast cars and lavish lifestyle, maintained too high a profile for success in the real world of espionage. In fiction, however, his high profile attracted a plethora of assassins, which added to the excitement. The novels and films were also remarkable for a stunning variety of gadgets, high-tech devices ranging from a weapon-studded sports car to tiny, rocket-equipped helicopters, all of which made for good reading and special effects in the films. Bond's women were both numerous and beautiful, and it's a tribute to Fleming's skill as a novelist that Bond found time for his official duties. Despite the distractions of women with unlikely names such as "Pussy Galore," Bond worked hard at his craft, which was that of a counter-espionage policeman, not a spy.

That's the real theme of the Bond novels. Bond was not a spy, despite the hype. He never ran a totally dark operation in enemy territory. His was always a defensive function, and Bond's superior brought him into the picture only after an enemy had stolen secret plans, a nuclear weapon, or otherwise endangered the security of the United Kingdom or its allies.

A darker picture came from John Le Carre, whose first spy novel was *The Spy Who Came in from the*

Cold. This was about a burned-out and disillusioned British agent who agreed to undertake one last mission before retiring, and who ended up shot to death trying to get back through the Iron Curtain. This cynical novel presented a British spymaster who sent his agent off with obsolete equipment, on a mission of doubtful value, so that he might maintain his standing among rival intelligence agencies. The theme was so compelling that it inspired a motion picture, starring Richard Burton and Claire Bloom.

Len Deighton was one of Le Carre's contemporaries, and he too presented a picture of betrayal and internal rot, beginning with his first book, *The Ipcress File.* His nameless agent worked for the Security Service, conducting routine surveillance, when a call from his boss led to his transfer to another smaller agency within the British intelligence establishment. This agency's chief turned out to be an arch-traitor, helping to mastermind a plot to kidnap and brainwash British scientists for the benefit of the Iron Curtain countries. Deighton followed this book with others, all following the same theme of wheels within wheels, and devious sub-plots. These books were so successful that several became motion pictures, starring Michael Caine as the agent, who had acquired the name "Harry Palmer" for the films.

Both Le Carre and Deighton showed the silly side of espionage: the bureaucratic back-biting and in-fighting that dilutes the efforts of their agents and administrators. It's silly, but not funny, because secret service executives are playing politics with people's lives and their country's security.

Walter Wager's novel, *Telefon*, is an example of imaginative use of "sleeper" agents. In this novel, later made into a motion picture starring Charles Bronson and Lee Remick, a Soviet espionage agency trains several dozen agents to pass as native Americans, and to take up residence in various parts of the United States. The imaginative twist is that these sleepers are not spies, but saboteurs. Each agent is to blend into American society and do absolutely nothing else until he or she gets a telephone call with the code phrase, "and miles to go before I sleep." Upon hearing this, the agent is to take from concealment a small, portable weapon, some of which are nuclear bombs, and proceed to the assigned target, where he detonates it, regardless of risk to himself. This was merely a contingency plan, for use in case of all-out war, but a renegade KGB officer decided to declare his own private war against the United States, and began activating the agents.

A similar theme dominated Brian Garfield's 1971 novel, *Deep Cover*. In this story, the Soviet Union operated a special facility, "Amergrad," built as a replica of an American town, to train infiltrators. In this town, everyone spoke English, the books and newspapers were American, all street and business signs were in English, and the population used American products and cars. A band of infiltrators slipped into the United States between 1954 and 1956, to take up residence in Arizona. One became a United States Representative, another an Air Force colonel, and yet others settled down around Tucson, near an Air Force ICBM installation. A renegade Soviet intelligence executive activated them to fire the missiles at Red China, a plot aborted at the last minute.

Art often imitates life. Some recent novels and motion pictures using the sleeper saboteur theme may have been inspired by the real-life example of Oleg Adolfovich Lyalin, a KGB officer stationed in Britain who defected in 1971. His cover, or open job, had been as a member of the Soviet Trading Delegation, while his secret function was working for the KGB. When he defected to the British, he revealed several Soviet plans for wide-spread sabotage in the United Kingdom, including destruction of radar installations.[1]

Frederick Forsyth's novel, *The Fourth Protocol*, appears to have been based loosely on this theme. The plot is that the KGB has sent an agent, fluent in English and familiar with the British lifestyle, to plant and detonate a small atom bomb next to an American air base in Britain, in violation of a secret fourth protocol to an arms-limitation treaty. The novel's success resulted in a motion picture, starring Michael Caine as the counter-espionage agent who uncovers the plot. The vicious twist in the plot is that the Soviet agent has a secret order to kill the technician who arrives to assemble the bomb after she completes her task, while she has a secret order to set the bomb's timer for instantaneous ignition, destroying him in the blast. This mutual destruction is to keep the bomb's origin totally secret, and make it appear as if an American bomb had accidentally exploded.

There have also been thousands of short stories with an espionage theme. At least two of Arthur Conan

Doyle's Sherlock Holmes stories, "The Adventure of the Bruce-Partington Plans," and "His Last Bow," dealt with espionage. Many 20th century authors have written spy stories, going outside their genre. Sax Rohmer, a writer of mystery stories, wrote "Blue Anemones." Edward D. Hoch, an American specializing in police procedurals, wrote "The People of the Peacock." Cornell Woolrich, another noted American mystery writer, wrote "Tokyo, 1941," a story about an American undercover agent in Japan arrested by the Japanese secret police, the "Kempei Tai," just before the Pearl Harbor attack.

With spy fiction so popular, satires were inevitable. Near the end of the series of James Bond novels, there appeared a few books featuring "Israel Bond," also known as "Agent Oy Oy Seven." A very successful TV series was *Get Smart*, starring Don Adams as the totally inept agent, Barbara Feldon as his beautiful female sidekick, and Edward Platt as the long-suffering "Chief." *Get Smart* focused on outlandish gadgets, such as a radio-telephone built into Agent Smart's shoe. There were weapons disguised as pens, cigarette lighters, and other common objects. Plots were ridiculous, enemies were stereotypes, and Agent Smart won every conflict despite his massive incompetence.

Fictional spies sometimes appear to be spying just for the fun of it. In real life, they do so for a variety of motives. Some motives are noble, while others are base. We'll study these next.

Sources

1. *Spyclopedia*, Richard Deacon, NY, Silver Arrow
   Books, 1988, pp. 329-330.

3

Motives

∞∞

People become spies for several reasons, and often two or more motives are operating simultaneously. Motives also can shift, and a spy who begins as an idealist can become very mercenary.

Adventure

Some people are bored with daily life, and find paper-shuffling and other routine work intolerable. They generate the excitement they crave by taking risks, such as driving fast, using drugs, or entering hazardous occupations. These are good recruits for wartime sabotage organizations, but can be liabilities in peacetime espionage. Their craving for action can lead them to take unnecessary chances.

Resentment

A person who is "mad at the world," or harbors a grudge against society in general and his country in particular, may be very destructive. He may shoot up a schoolyard with a semi-automatic rifle, or set fire to a crowded building. He may also betray his country, which is why some traitors have turned out to be conspicuous misfits.

We often find this sort of motive operating among members of ethnic or behavioral minorities. A minority group member may feel that his people have gotten a very raw deal in his country, and he may seek to sell out its secrets to a foreign power. The atomic spy ring, consisting of the Rosenbergs, their relatives, and associates, was one such case. Martin and Mitchell, employees of the National Security Agency who defected to Soviet Russia in 1960, were allegedly homosexuals. More recently, a Black state department official sold American classified information to an African power. Geoffrey Prime, who sold secrets stolen while he worked at the British cryptographic headquarters, was a child molester. He had gone through a successful ten-year career as a spy, and had retired from government service in 1978. Only the mishap of the Cheltenham police investigating him for a child molesting case caused his discovery, because a search of his home disclosed a cipher pad, and materials relating to micro-dots and other means of clandestine communication.[1]

Fear

Fear of consequences, or of one's future, can be a powerful motivator among defectors. Igor Gouzenko, for example, had made a serious error, which earned him a reprimand from his superior and the threat of recall to Moscow. This took place in 1945, during the no-nonsense Stalin era, when recall to Moscow could easily mean the firing squad or a labor camp. Gouzenko was a code clerk at the Russian Embassy, and he was so fearful of what might happen to him back in the U.S.S.R. that he purloined copies of messages to use as his admission ticket to Canada when he asked for asylum.

Fear for one's family is also a lever that spy recruiters use to manipulate potential agents. William Sebold, a naturalized American who had fought in the Kaiser's army during World War I, had relatives in Germany. He had emigrated to the United States, married, and started a family, supporting himself by working as a draftsman at the Consolidated Aircraft plant in San Diego, California. When he visited Germany in 1939, to see relatives he had left behind, Gestapo agents accosted him and took him to the Hamburg office. There, a Gestapo officer made it clear that the safety of his relatives in Germany depended on his cooperation. The Gestapo recruited him as an agent, trained him in espionage techniques, and shipped him off to America.

Sebold did not, however, serve Germany, as he reported his recruitment to American authorities and served as a double agent for almost two years.[2]

Ideology

This can be a powerful motivator. A spy or traitor may honestly believe that he or she is helping to create a better world by passing secrets to a more "progressive" society. This was a common motivator during the years before World War II, when Western countries were wracked by a depression, threatened by fascism, and the socialist countries promised a brighter day. A standard recruiting pitch by communist spy networks was to ask potential recruits if they wanted to "work for peace."[3] This was an all-purpose appeal, useful for gaining recruits for covert service and overt causes, such as nuclear disarmament, because it reflected the motives and aspirations of many people who had no connection with communist spy rings. In fact, "working for peace" became a catch-word of communist front organizations because of its wide appeal.

The "Cambridge Spy Ring" that passed a mountain of classified information to the Soviet Union was perhaps the best-known of this type. Young British aristocrats, disillusioned by their society's inequalities and their government's weak stand against Hitler and Mussolini, joined the underground delivering British secrets to Soviet agents. They worked their way up inside the government, helping each other attain sensitive positions, and presented their Soviet handlers with a very complete picture of Allied efforts during and after World War II. Also important among their motives was involvement with the homosexual network.[4]

Homosexuals have continued to spy. Another noted spy in Britain was John Vassal, a low-level employee in the Admiralty who had access to information the Soviets thought was worth purloining. Although he was not one of the Cambridge aristocrats, he passed many NATO secrets to a Soviet contact before the Security Service uncovered him.[5]

False-flag Recruiting

This term refers to recruiting a spy or traitor under false premises, because the handler feels that the prospective agent would not be receptive to working for him if he know his true employer. A common technique of false-flag recruiting is to tell the prospect that the handler is working for a friendly power. It may be necessary to assume the identity of a citizen of that country to reinforce the deception.

A German agent used the false-flag technique in recruiting Joseph Dugan, the technical operating chief of the U.S. State Department's code room in 1940. The German agent told Dugan that he was working for certain isolationist members of the U.S. Congress who wanted to keep an eye on the interventionists. Dugan was a committed isolationist, and the German agent convinced him that his contacts in Congress needed to know the contents of State department cables.[6]

Another example took place during the late 1950s, in Baltimore, Maryland. A Polish intelligence officer became friendly with an American who worked as a draftsman in a company which subcontracted for aircraft manufacturers. Although the American didn't handle any classified material, the Polish officer took the long view and felt that it was worth trying to develop him as a long-term agent, because he might someday be employed in classified work. He decided to get the American started in low-level work, and told him that he had a friend who worked for a German company. This "friend" needed blueprints of some American designs, especially those of aircraft parts, and was willing to pay. This made the offer appear to be for industrial espionage on behalf of a company in a friendly country.[7]

Another example took place in Mexico, again at the instigation of the Polish Intelligence Service. A Polish college professor who had fought in the Spanish Civil War, and who was fluent in both Spanish and French, sought out a career with the espionage service in Warsaw. Polish Intelligence officers calculated that it would be better to make this man over as a Frenchman, because he could pass for French. With the appropriate forged papers, the professor went to Mexico City, where the Polish Embassy had a clerk working undercover assignment, doing intelligence work. The professor encountered a Mexican engineering student named "Pedro," who had studied in the U.S. and was strongly anti-American. The professor saw that Pedro, despite his anti-Americanism, was not a communist, and would not take kindly to working for

a communist espionage service. His approach, therefore, was that he was a French Intelligence agent, who
was simply carrying out routine surveillance on an ally.
He explained to Pedro that allies do not always remain
allies, and often spy on each other just to be on the safe
side. Pedro agreed, and the plan was to infiltrate him
into the United States as a long-term project.

Pedro went to New York, to become a legal immi-
grant and eventually a naturalized citizen. The Polish
espionage service paid him a monthly retainer, to help
with his expenses, and held him in reserve, as he would
be a more valuable agent after becoming a citizen. The
ultimate objective was to have a Polish officer who
could pass for French service him, to continue the
illusion that he was working for France.[8]

Blackmail

It's almost trite to say that blackmailers are unethical, but in espionage, the lengths to which they will
go to frame someone are legendary. One young man,
Adam Kozicki, fell into the hands of an opportunistic
and unscrupulous intelligence officer when, shortly
after World War II, he found employment in Germany
as a guard assigned to Allied military posts. One night,
he fired a warning shot, which unfortunately struck a
British officer. Adam panicked, dropped his rifle, and
went to the Polish Repatriation Commission office.
There he found a Polish captain, and told him what
had happened. The captain, who worked for the Polish
Intelligence Service, sheltered Adam, and said that

he'd try to help him. He later returned to tell Adam that he was in real trouble, because the British officer had died. Actually, the bullet had only grazed the officer, and he didn't even file charges.

The captain told Adam that he could help him if Adam was willing to work for Polish intelligence. He had him sign a confession to the "murder," as a formality, and smuggled him back to Warsaw. Back in Poland, Adam underwent two years of intensive instruction in techniques of espionage, and how to pass as a citizen of the U.S. In 1950, he reported to a cover job as a crewman on the Polish ship "Batory," which was headed for New York. In New York Harbor, he jumped ship, and used false papers to assume his new cover as an American citizen. He worked for two years, until his recall to Warsaw in 1952.[9]

Anyone with a skeleton in his closet is vulnerable, and the spymaster's main effort is discovering people who have something to hide. Because of extensive security checks, it's unlikely that a potential recruit will have a criminal record unknown to his employer. More often, the secret has to do with current habits, such as gambling or sex. The compulsive gambler who owes more than he can cover isn't common in government service, but if a recruiter encounters one, he can make him "an offer he can't refuse," by giving him money and keeping his secret.

Sex is the other possibility. Government employees such as diplomats and cipher clerks have affairs, as do other people, and this can serve as a lever to manipulate them. Indeed, one of the main efforts of some espionage agencies is to set up situations to entrap people they wish to recruit. One such establishment, which received wide notoriety after World War II, was the Gestapo's "Salon Kitty," a high-class brothel for foreign diplomats. The German Security Service (Sicherheitsdienst) established a nine-bedroom brothel in a fashionable Berlin mansion, with microphones concealed in each bedroom. Madame Kitty, who directed the brothel, stated that diplomats and other high-level foreigners revealed enough during sessions with the prostitutes to make it worthwhile for the Germans to keep the operation running.[10]

A diplomat in a foreign post may be tempted to obtain sexual satisfaction from a native, if his wife isn't with him. An undiscovered homosexual will almost certainly go prowling on a foreign duty post. Even at home, he may leave himself open to blackmail.

During the 1950s, Polish intelligence officers encountered a West German businessman who appeared to be a good candidate for "honey-pot" entrapment. "Peter Schmidt" had built up an electronics firm and knew many German and American businessmen. He also had an eye for women, and the Polish recruiter arranged for him to meet "accidentally" a young Polish lady and have an affair. After several sexual encounters, Polish officers were ready to spring the trap. Schmidt was to meet the young lady at a resort in Poland during one of his trips, but she did not show up. Instead, two intelligence agents appeared, and confronted Schmidt with photographs and a tape recording of himself and the lady in compromising positions. As Schmidt was married, this amounted to blackmail. The two officers demanded that Schmidt pass electronic designs to them, as well as help them plant their agents in German companies. They also wanted him to provide information on the personal characteristics and weaknesses of other German industrialists who might be good recruiting prospects. Schmidt agreed, at first, but killed himself shortly thereafter.[11]

The "honey-pot" recruitment was probably more common years ago than it is today, because attitudes towards sex were less tolerant then. Still, today there are set-ups for vulnerable people, such as the Marine Guards at the Moscow embassy. Attractive young women, in the employ of the KGB, took advantage of the needs of these lusty young men assigned to lonely foreign duty.

In one sense, the stupidity of the American Government set these marines up for exploitation. Allowing marines to serve in what amounts to social isolation for many months is leaving them vulnerable, and it would not have been difficult to devise some safety valves, such as allowing them to bring wives or girl-friends with them to Moscow. However, the moralistic attitude of the government sometimes rivals that of the Roman Catholic Church, and government administrators totally ignore reality.

Likewise Richard Miller, father of eight, who allowed himself to fall for Svetlana Ogorodnikov, the Soviet agent already discussed. Miller was perhaps at his most vulnerable, a middle-aged family man who had seen his youth slip away.

Homosexual contact leaves the participant open to blackmail, even today. At the turn of the century, it was practically the kiss of death. This may be how Colonel Alfred Redl, of the Austrian General Staff, became embroiled in spying against his country. Whatever the original motive, Redl was soon collecting money for his services to the Russian Secret Service, and the method of payment eventually led to his undoing.[12] A description of Redl's activities was written in 1928, and contains euphemisms and allusions that suggest what it was impolite to say directly. A paragraph describing how Redl began his career as a spy states that a Russian nobleman came to "gay" Vienna, and that Redl made Vienna still more "gay" for him. The Russian apparently was a figure in his country's clandestine service, and was ready to propose a deal with Redl. They went for a walk in the country, and when they were alone, found that they "psychologically and spiritually spoke the same language." After several hours, "they understood each other very well." With this elliptical language, the author makes it clear that Redl's treason began with a homosexual intrigue involving a Russian spymaster/seducer, although it's not at all clear who seduced whom.

The theme of homosexual blackmail has continued through the years. Although the English upper class has developed a generations-old reputation for homosexuality, as promoted in the all-male schools which they traditionally attend, there's still enough intolerance in British society to keep homosexuals worried that their secret vice may come to light. One example was the blackmail of Donald Maclean by his close "friend," Guy Burgess, in 1941. Maclean was bisexual, and one of his contacts was Burgess, who got him drunk and set him up with another man, in a nude scene which he photographed. This was additional leverage to ensure his loyalty to the Soviet spy ring.[13]

Anthony Blunt, the British "Fourth Man," was a homosexual himself. He also used homosexual blackmail to lubricate the wheels of his spy ring and keep members cooperative.[14]

Homosexuals are prone to betray their homelands, sometimes because of resentment, and at other times because of blackmail. This is why security officers try to weed out homosexuals from sensitive positions. It's not a matter of "homophobia," but practicality, based on extensive experience and documented through the years.

Extortion

Closely allied to blackmail is extortion. Anyone with relatives abroad, where the foreign power attempting espionage can reach them, is vulnerable to this approach. This is how the Gestapo recruited William Sebold.

A representative of the foreign power informs the prospective spy that his family's welfare and safety depend upon the information he can provide. This is an almost irresistible appeal, which is why governments routinely deny security clearances to anyone with relatives living in countries under control of hostile powers.

Espionage services use extortion not only to recruit spies, but to keep them in line. Ernest Oldham, a British Foreign Office employee, was a code clerk who was one of the Soviets' earliest recruits. His original motive was money. In 1929, after not getting a pay raise he'd anticipated, he went to the Russian Embassy in Paris to offer his services.[15]

Oldham not only passed secret information to the Russians, but recruited at least one more agent for them, Captain John Herbert King, also a code clerk. In 1932, Oldham decided to get out, but his control officer objected. Despite this, Oldham resigned from his job, making the Russians nervous that he would endanger their other agents. In September, 1933, Oldham fell victim to coal gas asphyxiation in his kitchen in London, with an official verdict of "suicide." Unofficially, this may have been the work of the Russian dirty tricks department.[16]

Conflicting or Dual Loyalties

Anyone coming from, or with relatives in a foreign country may be vulnerable to this. A wish to help the other country may result simply from a stronger loyalty.

During World War II, for example, there was special concern regarding German, Italian, and Japanese immigrants. In fact, the Japanese espionage service recruited informers from the many Japanese and Japanese-descent persons in Hawaii. This information helped in planning the Pearl Harbor attack. Although civil libertarians condemn the mass round-up of Japanese in the United States that took place immediately after Pearl Harbor, there were many Japanese who held dual loyalties, and some did, in fact, collect information for the Japanese government.

Before the war, the German-American Bund was openly supportive of Hitler and the Nazi regime. Although this organization comprised only a tiny percentage of German-Americans, some of its members and affiliates were dangerous because of their loyalty to Germany, and the government interned them when war began. It's standard practice to intern enemy aliens at the outbreak of war, and in both Britain and the United States, citizens of enemy countries found themselves behind barbed wire after mass round-ups.

Jews throughout the world feel an affinity for Israel, and many Jews openly raise funds for the Israeli government. They buy Israeli bonds, and even conduct collections for special purposes, such as schools and orphanages. In the United States, there is a registered Israeli lobby, AIPAC (American-Israeli Political Action Committee) which provides campaign contributions to legislators in return for support of Israel and Israeli interests. AIPAC also organizes opposition to legislators who don't take the Israeli side, and some of its members organize letter-writing campaigns to label as "anti-Semitic" anyone who opposes a pro-Israeli policy.

Loyalty to Israel can also involve helping that country's clandestine services. In Egypt, a clandestine Israeli-run network recruited its members "from the

ranks of local Jewish organizations."[17] These, including
Eli Cohen, who later ended his life on a Syrian gallows
for espionage, formed a sabotage group. In 1954, they
sabotaged British and American installations.

During the search for Adolf Eichmann, Israel's
secret service used the services of Jews living in
Europe and South America. In Germany, a Jew in the
office of the Public Prosecutor passed information
regarding Eichmann to the Israelis.[18] In South America, Jews from several countries joined in the search
for the Eichmann family. Isser Harel, who at the time
was head of the Israeli Secret Service, stated that
during the Eichmann capture there was no "local
body" to help the team sent to do the job.[19] It's true
that there was no formal organization of Jews that
stood ready to help the Israeli secret service, but
individuals were constantly available. Throughout his
account, Harel mentions Jews living in several South
American countries who performed reconnaissances
and provided other services for the team sent from
Israel. Harrel is careful not to mention real names, and
he conceals enough details to make it difficult to
discover who these helpful Jews are. One obvious
reason is to protect them from reprisals at the hands
of Nazis and Nazi sympathizers living in South American countries.

In the Pollard case, a U.S. Navy intelligence analyst
of Jewish background passed many classified documents to Israeli agents. This was, according to his own
statement, simply out of loyalty to Israel, although he
accepted large sums of money for the information. The
Israeli government promoted the idea that he'd be-

trayed his country for mercenary reasons, to minimize the incident's kicking back against other American Jews.[20]

Money

This is a very common motive, especially in peacetime, when the risk of the death penalty is less. The Walker spy ring operated for two decades, from the middle 1960s to the 1980s, all for money. Ideology was irrelevant, as it was for the "Falcon and Snowman," and others who sold secrets for pay.

Money, or the need for money, has long been a key to recruiting agents. Professional spymasters understand this, and make the most of it. The Soviets learned that, unlike their idealistic left-wing predecessors, American spies in recent years have been in it for the money. However, money has always played a role in espionage.

During the early years of German espionage in the United States, the Abwehr had an agent planted in a loan company in Washington, DC, to report on American military officers in debt, because these were potential recruits.[21] This was a very clever method of "talent-spotting," because the German agent was not normally vulnerable to a security check, as he would have been in government employ. Further, private credit information is not classified by the government, and this reduced the agent's criminal liability if ever caught.

One energetic German agent used a shotgun approach, mailing letters to American officers informing them that they could earn money easily by contacting the writer. The method used was placing an ad in the *New York Times* classified section. The letters also contained warnings against reporting their contents to the American Intelligence Services. However, at least one naval ensign turned over the letter to his superiors.[22]

Sometimes, debt-ridden spies recruit themselves. David Barnett, who had been a CIA agent from 1958 to 1970, decided to go into business for himself. He started an import-export business in Indonesia, where he had been stationed, but encountered financial hard times. He approached the Soviets and sold them the names of about thirty CIA agents and contacts in Indonesia and the Far East. He also revealed to the Soviets how CIA agents had infiltrated the Indonesian Navy, which used Soviet SA-2 anti-aircraft missiles, and how this led to the development of American counter-measures against these missiles. He also acted as a talent spotter for the Soviets, furnishing information about CIA employees he thought would make good prospects for recruitment. This earned him $92,600 in payment.[23]

At times, it appears that espionage agencies are lavish with money, making copious payments to their spies, but in reality they operate within budgets, as do other government departments. In fact, espionage agencies are very cheap. Roderick James Ramsey, a former U.S. Army sergeant who had access to NATO nuclear plans, sold his information to Eastern Bloc agents for only $20,000, according to his statement to the FBI. During a preliminary hearing, an FBI agent testified that he knew of no other case involving so much information passed at one time, and that the Eastern Bloc now had all of our plans.[24]

Ramsey was part of an operation run by Clyde Lee Conrad, who was convicted of treason in a West German court on June 6, 1990. Conrad's ring had passed a variety of classified NATO information to Hungarian and Czechoslovakian intelligence agents, collecting a total of between $2 million and $5 million for it.

The notorious Falcon and Snowman case was typical of espionage for money. Christopher Boyce, former Catholic altar boy and the son of an FBI Agent, obtained a job at TRW Systems Group. His assignment was in a highly classified installation which processed signals from American surveillance satellites and their ground control stations. Boyce and a close friend, Andrew Daulton Lee, who dabbled in dope, decided that they could earn large amounts of money passing secrets to the Soviets. Lee went to Mexico City, where the Soviet Embassy runs operations against the United States, and presented his offer. Soviet officials, with the experience of many walk-ins under their belts, were cautious at first, but after checking out the microfilms Lee had brought with him, decided to buy more. Boyce and Lee collected at least $70,000 from the Soviets for the documents they passed over, before Mexican police caught Lee throwing material over the fence into the Soviet compound.[25]

Perhaps the most successful, and most damaging, spy ring working for any motive was the Walker Spy Ring. John Walker, a U.S. Navy petty officer who had access to navy codes, sold his country's crypto secrets to the Soviets for about two decades. John Walker's motive was simply monetary, and his income from spying boosted his standard of living.

The consequences of the Walker Ring's efforts were far-reaching. One hitherto unexplained event was the attack upon an American electronic intelligence ship, the U.S.S. Liberty, by Israeli warplanes and warships in June, 1967, during the Six-Day War. The Liberty was stationed in international waters, off the Israeli coast, when the war broke out. The ship's crew were monitoring Israeli radio traffic, and relaying the information to the National Security Agency in Washington. Israeli aircraft and warships strafed and shot up the Liberty until the transmissions stopped. Afterward, the Israeli government apologized for the attack, which was allegedly a "mistake," although it took place in broad daylight.

The motive for the attack was clear, despite the Israeli explanation. It was to stop the monitoring of their radio traffic, and the relaying of information to Washington, because the Israelis knew that the Soviets were reading American naval machine ciphers. This information probably came from a spy inside the Soviet Union, probably someone of Jewish background who felt that his primary loyalty was to Israel, not to his homeland.

An additional complication came from the instructions given to Walker by his Soviet control officers, who told him that they did not need any information on one type of cryptographic machine. Presumably, the Soviets already had one or more agents inside the U.S. government who had provided this information.

Richard Miller was the first FBI Agent to be convicted of espionage. His motive was a desperate need for money, as he had eight children and was in debt.[26] This made him very vulnerable to a monetary approach, although there was a bit of "honey-pot" in it as well. He had an extra-marital affair with Svetlana Ogorodnikov, a Soviet national who had arrived in the United States with her husband in 1973. Svetlana apparently also introduced Miller, a Mormon, to strong liquor, and propositioned him to spy for the Soviet Union.[27]

The yearning for money sometimes results in a spy's selling bogus information, or misrepresenting the information he sells to his controls. There have been countless instances of "spies" manufacturing information, or culling newspapers and magazines for information not available in the country for which they're working, and compiling reports based upon the news. After the end of World War II, a horde of fakers descended upon Western intelligence services with "information" about the Red Army to sell. Sometimes this was pure fabrication. Other information was the embellishment of accounts from refugees. A favorite ploy was to contact a Western intelligence agency, claiming to represent a "friend" who was in a high position with the Soviet military or intelligence branches, and offer information. Naturally, the friend's identity could not be disclosed, to protect him.[28]

Some bogus agents still try this tactic. This is why the competent spyhandler runs two or more agents on the same project.

At times, spyhandlers promise to pay an agent large amounts of money, but do not put it into his hands. Correctly pointing out that having a large amount of money would be dangerous, they propose to make periodic deposits in a Swiss numbered account, or defer payments following another plan. If the spy is caught, they never have to pay off, and they merely withdraw the money. This is why anyone spying for money ought to begin worrying if there's any sort of deferred payment plan. The more his handler owes him, the greater the temptation to turn him in to avoid paying. A spyhandler can be as greedy and unethical as a used car salesman.

If you're selling secrets for money, you should always get the money immediately, without fail, and not accept I.O.U.s. For your own safety, have a way of rat-holing the payments planned in advance, and be sure never to tell your control agent exactly what you're doing with the funds.

At times, agents embezzle money received for use in carrying out their missions. When funds are secret and unvouchered, they're wide-open for theft, and abuses probably occur far more often than the taxpayers know.

One common dodge, which begins as a way of building a cover, is to start a business. If the business is anemic, the spy agency will subsidize it to maintain their agent's cover. On the other hand, if the business is profitable, the agent can divert part of the profits for his own purposes. Building a retirement fund is one end-use. The agent may assume that, once the spy agency has no further use for him, they'll throw him out to sink or swim economically, and this appears to be standard practice among espionage agencies except for American ones.

Yet another use for profits generated by cover companies is to provide funds for super-secret projects, some of which may be totally unauthorized. Governments feel that, because they ultimately control the purse strings, they can keep their clandestine services under tight control, and prevent them from creating policy on their own. This is a comforting delusion, because control of clandestine services depends mainly upon the wish of operatives to submit to control.

A cover company, such as "Air America," is actually a private corporation, started with seed money from secret funds, but growing larger by re-investing its profits. Air America operated for years under contract to the U.S. Air Force and other government agencies, to earn the money it needed to support other operations.[29]

The problem comes when company executives invest profits into other totally unknown businesses, to create new profit centers. Some of these businesses are open, with only their connection to espionage operatives secret. There are also others that are totally illegal. There have been rumors for years that the CIA was in the illegal drug business, for example. Although it appears far-fetched, it would be perfectly practical to use CIA channels, with their exemption from customs inspection, to smuggle illicit drugs or other contraband. It's totally unknown to the public whether the CIA used these profits for agency purposes, or private ones.

Sources

1. *Mask of Treachery*, John Costello, NY, Warner Books, 1988, p. 580.

2. *Nazi Spies in America*, William Breuer, NY, St. Martin's Press, 1989, pp. 142-150.

3. *Spycatcher*, Peter Wright, NY, Dell Books, 1987, p. 313.

4. *Mask of Treachery*. This entire book is interspersed with references to the deeply-seated and active homosexual network at Cambridge and elsewhere, which became involved in spying for the Soviets.

5. *Ibid.*, p. 549.

6. *Nazi Spies in America*, p. 162.

7. *Spy in the U.S.*, Pawel Monat, NY, Berkley Books, 1961, pp. 151-158.

8. *Ibid.*, pp. 164-165.

9. *Ibid.*, pp. 176-178.

10. *Spyclopedia*, Richard Deacon, NY, Silver Arrow Books, 1988, pp. 234-235.

11. *Spy in the U.S.*, pp. 166-170.

12. *The Fine Art of Spying*, Edited by Walter B. Gibson, NY, Tempo Books, 1967, article by Joseph Gollomb, pp. 159-185.

13. *Spyclopedia*, p. 167.

14. *Mask of Treachery*, p. 24.

15. *Ibid.*, pp. 160-161.

16. *Spyclopedia*, pp. 222-223.

17. *Decline of Honor*, Avri El-Ad, Chicago, Henry Regnery Company, 1976, p. 125.

18. *The House on Garibaldi Street*, Isser Harel, NY, Viking Press, 1975, p. 3.

19. *Ibid.*, p. 78.

   See also: *By Way of Deception*, Victor Ostrovsky, NY, St. Martin's Press, 1990, pp. 86-88. The Israeli espionage service, the Mossad, has a network of "sayanim," Jews who work part-time for the Israelis, scattered throughout the world. Among the Jews in London, England, about 2,000 are active helpers who provide support to Israeli agents. Sayanim rent cars and apartments, doctors among them treat bullet wounds without asking questions, and others provide funds. Sayanim also provide business addresses to support an agent's cover, all without recompense.

20. *Territory of Lies*, Wolf Blitzer, NY, Harper Paperbacks, 1989, p. 279.

21. *Nazi Spies in America*, p. 37.

22. *Ibid.*, p. 71.

23. *Merchants of Treason*, Thomas B. Allen and Norman Polmar, NY, Dell Books, 1988, pp. 204-205.

24. Associated Press, June 9, 1990.

25. *Merchants of Treason*, pp. 205-206.

26. *Spyclopedia*, p. 337.

27. *Merchants of Treason*, pp. 267-276.

28. *Mole*, William Hood, NY, Ballantine Books, 1983, p. 16.

29. *The Secret Team*, L. Fletcher Prouty, NY, Ballantine Books, 1974, pp. 312-314.

4

Recruiting Spies

<hr>

There's been a lot of nonsense written about recruiting spies, and the qualities spymasters seek in secret agents. They're supposed to be keen observers, with almost photographic memories, in good physical shape, and even masters of judo, karate, and other martial arts.

Real-life spies are less flamboyant. In real life, there are usually only two kinds of people who get recruited into the business; bureaucrats who obey orders, and people with access to vital information. There are certain exceptions, such as the adventurers recruited during wartime when sabotage becomes necessary.

The bureaucrats are the control officers, or "handlers," who recruit and direct the agents. Espionage organizations also recruit low-level service personnel, such as couriers and "cut-outs." The courier is actually expendable, and his role is to expose himself and take the risks by ferrying messages and sensitive material past control points in enemy territory. Often, he won't even know who passed the material to him, because he picks it up by servicing a "dead drop," where an agent drops off material for later pick-up. This is why he's sometimes called a "cut-out." If security officers capture the courier, he can't reveal the identities of his contacts.

Another type of service worker is the operator of a "safe house," a refuge for the spy in enemy territory. The safe house owner or operator only knows that, from time to time, he'll have to accommodate people who need a place to stay. He doesn't need to know their identities or their roles. Still, if the counter-espionage police arrest a safe house operator, he faces the same penalties as a full-fledged spy or agent.

It's possible to recruit a master spy who speaks ten languages, has photographic recall, is a master of disguise, a crack shot, and who can impersonate almost anyone as he infiltrates to a sensitive position. Such exceptional people are very rare, and it's much easier to recruit the loser who already occupies a sensitive job, and to milk him for everything he knows. If you're in the business of spotting potential spies, or recruiting them, you'll be looking for someone with money problems whom you can seduce into trading secrets for cash. You also need to look at people who love lavish lifestyles, but don't have the earning power to support them. You'll also be looking for someone with a very unhappy situation, such as a wife he hates, or an insecure job. This type is a potential defector, and if you can persuade him to leave his problems behind and come over to your side with a suitcase full of secrets, you'll have done your job well.

This shows the irony of espionage. The most valuable information in peacetime comes from people who are in sensitive jobs, with access to secret information, not from taxi drivers and street-sweepers. To obtain such a job, it's first necessary to pass a security check, and therefore the only people today who can betray their countries' secrets are those who have passed security checks.

Walk-ins

This is the simplest way of recruiting a spy. A foreign national walks into your embassy or consulate and tells you he has something to sell. If he's genuine, he may be worth a lot to your country. If he's a fake, you stand to lose a lot. If he's selling bogus information you can pay a lot of cash for trash. If he's a provocateur, he may be setting you up for an arrest, or worse.

A spyhandler who accepts a foreign citizen's offer of secrets for sale takes a risk, especially if he doesn't check him out carefully first. This is why a person who walks in through the front door may get rebuffed.

If you agree to meet someone on a street corner, you may receive a briefcase full of classified documents, but under photographic surveillance. Once you take the briefcase, and hand over a package of money, plainclothes police close in and make the arrest.

There's often a period of testing, to build up a picture of the walk-in's value and his reliability. The case officer may instruct him to procure unclassified information at first, simply to determine if the volunteer is truthful and prompt. This buys time for the spymaster's undercover sources inside the country to check the walk-in carefully, to determine if he really is who he says. Sometimes, a superficial check will show that the walk-in is a member of the counter-espionage police.

A member of the legation may go to the walk-in's alleged address, and ask a neighbor when the "FBI Agent" will be home. A walk-in known to his neighbors as an FBI Agent is automatically suspect, unless he's already stated that he is with the FBI. More likely, the neighbor may disclose that the walk-in has been at that address for only a few weeks, a definite "caution" sign.

Front Members

Espionage organizations also recruit workers from "front" organizations. A front may be a cultural, religious, social, or political organization, and it often serves as a pool of raw material for the espionage organization. Some fronts are started by and under the total control of the parent espionage organization, but most are simply groups of people with a common ethnic or ideological affiliation. Although the organization's founder may not have intended it to serve the espionage service as a recruiting base, in practice it often happens. If you're the newly-assigned control officer in an embassy, the first place you look for potential recruits is the front organization's membership list.

The German-American Bund was such an organization. So is the Communist Party. The "Comintern," or Communist International, was an organization directed from Moscow, with the purpose of uniting people who were attracted to the Communist ideology anywhere in the world. Communist Parties sprang up in many countries, all supported and directed by Moscow. The Comintern also served another purpose from the start.

That purpose was talent-spotting and recruitment. From their early days, Communist espionage organizations were very adept and professional about recruitment, and they made a massive effort that paid off very well.

Membership in the Communist Party could be a handicap, because of background checks conducted by security agents on anyone applying for a sensitive position. Therefore, many talent-spotters discouraged potential agents from joining the Communist Party. One recruiter was Tom Black, a party member who recruited Harry Gold, a courier for the Rosenberg ring. Gold, being poor and Jewish during the 1930s, grew up to be a left-wing sympathizer.[1]

He felt that Soviet Russia held promise for the people of the world, and particularly for Jews, because official Communist policy did not tolerate anti-Semitism. Indeed, many Russian Jews sided with the Communist cause during the revolution, and many of the top Soviet officials, such as Trotsky, Kaganovich and Litvinov, were Jewish.[2] With this background, Gold was prepared to serve his cause, rather than his country.

Gold was not the only one. There are many Jewish names in the list of American-born traitors passing information to the Soviet Union. David Greenglass, who was Julius Rosenberg's brother-in-law, was one. Judith Coplon was another. Harry Dexter White was also Jewish, but had a WASP-sounding name because he had changed it.

In 1933, Tom Black got Gold a job with a soap-manufacturing company, an act of kindness which Gold appreciated because the country was in the Great Depression and jobs were scarce. Black tried to get Gold to join the Communist Party, but Gold hesitated. In 1935, Gold got another job, with the Pennsylvania Sugar Company, and Black persuaded Gold to turn over various secret industrial processes to him.[3] During World War II, Harry Gold worked as a courier, and one of his major efforts was making a trip to Albuquerque and Santa Fe, New Mexico, to convey secret nuclear bomb information from David Green-glass and Klaus Fuchs to Julius Rosenberg.[4]

Julius and Ethel Rosenberg were New Yorkers who had joined the Communist Party. They faithfully supported the party politically, and did some underground work for it. Starting in 1940 and through World War II, Julius Rosenberg worked as a civilian employee for the U.S. Army Signal Corps, but the Army belatedly fired him in 1945 as a security risk, because of his Communist views. During this time, Rosenberg was part of a spy ring, and had boasted to his brother-in-law, David Greenglass, that he headed a network of spies all over the United States.[5]

One problem with members of front organizations is that counter-espionage police probably know their identities, and are keeping them under surveillance. Membership in a front organization is usually disqualification for any sort of employment requiring a security clearance. Still, if you're building a network, don't overlook front organizations. These can provide couriers and cut-outs, as well as safe houses.

Another danger is that counter-spies usually infiltrate front organizations, to obtain an inside view of their operations. Running infiltrators is exactly like running spies, but in certain ways it's easier. Police agents may persuade a member, against whom they have criminal charges, that it's in his best interest to work for them. In return for having the charges dropped, the "turned" member reports on the organization. He reports on the events at meetings, supplies lists of members, and any other information he can gather. If you're using front organization members in your spy network, you must always keep in mind that you may have recruited a leak, and you should never allow a front member to occupy a crucial position in your network.

Family Ties

Just as Julius Rosenberg recruited his brother-in-law, other spies began their careers because of family influence. One of the most damaging spies for Britain was George Blake, who while assigned to British Intelligence in Germany betrayed 42 British agents and the Berlin Tunnel to the Soviets. Blake's name when he was born was "George Behar," an Egyptian Jew whose uncle, Henri Curiel, participated in founding the Egyptian Communist Party in 1943. Blake apparently was assigned as a sleeper agent at first, because he joined the Royal Navy as a seaman, later becoming an officer. He had graduated to intelligence work for the Secret Intelligence Service when he became a prisoner of the North Koreans. This crucial detail led to the misapprehension that Blake had suffered brainwashing at the hands of the North Koreans, obscuring his communist sympathies which dated from an earlier age.[6]

Behar/Blake was an "infiltrator," and the term "mole" would apply very well to him. As a foreigner, he worked his way into the British Intelligence Service, where he did his damage.

Another infiltrator who was phenomenally successful was "Larry" Wu-Tai Chin, a Peking-born agent who successfully infiltrated the CIA and secretly worked for the People's Republic of China for 33 years. From his first job with the U.S. Consulate in Shanghai, he reported back to his Peking masters. He continued to rise in the CIA, becoming an intelligence analyst. He retired in 1981, but did freelance jobs for the CIA. The FBI, our much-overrated counter-espionage agency, placed a tap on his telephone, but did not inform the CIA, which continued to employ him. Although he was a low-level employee, he had access to high-level secrets, and smuggled out many documents for photocopying and transmittal to China.[7]

Defectors

These are related to walk-ins, but are of two types. The simple defector is the person who leaves his country, and comes over physically to the other side. He doesn't come over simply begging for asylum, but has something to trade. This may be memorized information, or it may be a sheaf of valuable documents, as Igor Gouzenko lifted from the code room of the Soviet Embassy when he came over to the Canadians in 1945. Belenko, the Soviet pilot who flew a MIG-25 to Japan as his admission ticket to the United States, gave U.S. Air Force officers several days' look at this jet fighter before they handed it back to the Soviets.

The defector-in-place is the traitor who gives his loyalty to another country, but remains at his sensitive job to pass information or documents over to his new employer. Jonathan Jay Pollard was a defector-in-place, who felt that his primary loyalty lay with Israel instead of the country of his birth. Kim Philby was another.

Some defectors are high-ranking officers. Leon Feldbin, an NKVD official who defected to the United States in 1938, used the name of "General Alexander Orlov," and reconstructed some of his training materials for the American government.[8]

One individual who almost fit the role of defector was General Reinhard Gehlen, who had been head of the Third Reich's Eastern front military intelligence operation. As Germany was being defeated in 1945, Gehlen was simply taking the most expedient route for self-preservation in surrendering. To avoid being treated as a POW or refugee, he gave himself to the Americans in 1945 with all his files, offering his network of agents in the Eastern zone as the price for good treatment. Gehlen understood that American military officers felt that war with the Soviet Union was imminent, and that they were in desperate need of a network of agents in Eastern Europe.[9]

There's a certain protocol defectors and their hosts follow, to extract the most from the relationship. First, the defector knows that he must have something to sell or trade. If you try to defect, but come over empty-handed asking for asylum, you're merely an exile, refugee, or displaced person. To get your hosts' attention, and the status and special treatment you expect, you must have valuable information, in your head or in your pockets. This is normal procedure for any defector except those so high-ranking that their defection is a propaganda coup for the host country. A famous artist, statesman, or writer is so prestigious that his defection produces very negative P.R. for the country he flees.

The defector's new hosts will offer him hospitality, usually including shelter, food, housekeeping, and entertainment. There may also be bodyguards to protect him from reprisals from his mother country's "special action" service. The hosts may wish to use him for propaganda, which is why he must have the sensitivity and guile to tell them what they want to hear. They may expect him to make a public statement that he came over because he sought freedom from the oppression in his country. To retain credibility, he must not mention any other relevant circumstances, such as gambling debts, a failing marriage, or a dead-end career.

His hosts will typically keep the defector in a safe house within their own country, completely apart from any other facility of the intelligence organization. They'll spend many hours debriefing him, to extract as much information as possible while it's still fresh. At the outset, however good the defector appears to be, his hosts will have a guarded attitude towards him. They'll suspect that he might be a plant, or that he might not know as much as he claims. A team of interrogators will squeeze every morsel of information possible from him, not only for immediate use, but also to build up a picture of the organization in which the defector had served.

The defector may have to undergo a polygraph examination. This requirement varies greatly, depending upon both the host country and the particular situation. The American CIA appears to believe in the polygraph, and its agents "flutter" any defector they can. The Israelis also place great faith in the polygraph, both for criminal and national-security investigations. The polygraph, however, is an unreliable instrument, and its successes come mainly from intimidating a naive subject into confessing the truth.

One outstanding example of the polygraph's failure was in the case of Robert McFarlane, White House National Security Advisor during the Reagan Administration. At one point, the *New York Times* published an article which indicated that someone in the White House had "leaked" the information. Investigators pressured McFarlane into submitting to the polygraph twice, and he flunked each time. In desperation, McFarlane asked the *New York Times'* management to tell the White House that he had not been the source of the leak. The publisher of the *Times* did consent to tell the President that his advisor had not been the source for that leak, and this backed up McFarlane's contention of innocence.[10]

The decision regarding use of the polygraph depends a lot on practical circumstances. A defector-in-place is in no position to go to CIA headquarters for a polygraph examination. Although the CIA does have traveling interrogation teams, who bring their polygraph with them, they cannot operate freely everywhere in the world. At times, using the polygraph is out of the question. If, however, the defector-in-place travels to a country friendly to the United States, or even a neutral one, a team can be on hand to "flutter" him. The defector who physically comes over also puts himself within reach of a flutter team. Interrogation with drugs is also possible, and even likely, if his hosts have absolute control over him. The defector does not, in practice, have any "rights," since he is not a citizen.

There have been severe failures in polygraph tests the CIA gives defectors who come over to the United States. The former Director of Central Intelligence, William Casey, told William Safire of the *New York Times* that a competent spy could fool the machine with "Valium and a few tricks."[11]

Given this, it's not surprising that the "information" derived from various Soviet defectors has been confusing and contradictory. It's almost certain that the KGB sent "plants," or fake defectors, over to the West to undo the harm that genuine defectors had done, and to generally confuse the picture. Any competent intelligence service would have been negligent not to try to do this. The procedure for selecting candidates for this ticklish assignment is fairly simple. It's only necessary to conduct a seminar in techniques of fooling the polygraph, and then test students to determine which has the necessary ability.

An example was Yuri Nosenko, an alleged high-level KGB officer who defected in 1964 with controversial information. He alleged that the KGB had had nothing to do with Lee Harvey Oswald, President Kennedy's assassin, although Oswald had married the niece of a KGB general while living in the Soviet Union. He also cast doubts on the information obtained from Oleg Penkovsky, a GRU officer who was a defector-in-place for British and American spy organizations.

James Angleton, CIA counter-intelligence chief at the time, was so suspicious of Nosenko that he ordered him drugged and kept incommunicado for three and a half years.[12] One sharp suspicion Angleton had about Nosenko was that his real purpose was to direct attention away from a high-level Soviet mole in the CIA.[13] There were grounds for doubting Nosenko's stories, but not everyone was as adamant as Angleton, who became a very controversial character within the CIA because of his incessant suspiciousness. William Colby, when he became Director of Central Intelligence, had Angleton resign.

Another defector who was probably a fake was Vitali Yurchenko, who defected to the United States in 1985. One of his services to the CIA was fingering several of its employees as Soviet agents. However, within a few months Yurchenko slipped away from his CIA escort while dining at a French restaurant only a few blocks from the Russian Embassy in Washington. He then re-defected to the Soviets. At a press conference, he accused the CIA of kidnaping, drugging, and torturing him.[14]

Interrogators will cross-check everything the defector tells them against what they already know, trying to spot gaps and inconsistencies that might indicate a plant. They'll scrutinize carefully any new knowledge he brings, calculating the odds that it's genuine. Over weeks, or months, they'll form an opinion regarding the defector's truthfulness and value to their side. This will count heavily in deciding his subsequent fate. A genuine defector with valuable information can get anything he wishes, within reason, from his host. This includes a stipend, employment, and even prostitutes for his sexual enjoyment. If the defector is genuine, he'll receive extensive help in "relocation," assuming a new identity and finding a home in the host country where the assassins of his motherland's "special action" service won't find him.

Attempting to defect to the other side holds a special hazard if the other side is already infiltrated. Konstantin Volkov, a Soviet national and NKVD Agent who attempted to defect to the British in 1945, found this out the hard way. He turned up one day at the British embassy in Istanbul, and announced his intention to come over. He stated to the British Secret Service resident that he knew the names of some Soviet agents in Britain, and offered to inform the British in return for asylum. He insisted that the news of his impending defection not go out over the normal cable traffic, because the Soviet Union had agents within British Intelligence and within the foreign office. The SIS station chief, Cyril Machray, sent a written message via diplomatic courier, but unfortunately the matter ended up on the desk of Kim Philby, one of those Volkov had been trying to avoid.[15]

Philby knew that if Volkov ever made it to the British Isles, where he'd undergo an extensive debriefing, he would expose Philby's true allegiance. Philby therefore delayed taking action on the impending defection, stalling while he got the news to his Russian control, Boris Kotrov. By the time Philby finally arrived in Istanbul, a couple of weeks later, Volkov had disappeared. There was a report of two persons strapped to stretchers, apparently Volkov and his wife, taken aboard a Russian military aircraft, which had then left immediately for the Soviet Union.[16]

Some defectors find themselves inadequately protected by the other side's intelligence service, or even cut loose because of a credibility problem. It may also be that the information they bring simply has little value. A Polish Jew named Ginsberg, who took the name Walter Krivitsky when he joined the GRU, decided that the Stalin purge might catch up to him. Thus, he defected to the West in 1937, and tried to get Western security services to accept his story that there were Soviet penetration agents in key positions in most of their agencies. Some of the information he provided checked out, but a lot was ignored. He also testified before the Dies Committee of the U.S. Congress. The dirty tricks section of the Soviet apparatus has a long arm, and Krivitsky died of an apparently self-inflicted gunshot wound in a Washington, D.C. hotel on February 10, 1941. As in the Oldham case, an arranged suicide is one of the ways assassins get rid of their victims.[17]

The defector-in-place eventually wants to go "home," to the country which he's been secretly serving for months or years. The promise of asylum is often the most important promise an agent handler can make to the defector, but whether he will ever fulfill this promise is another matter. When an agent is passing valuable information, his control is reluctant to shut down the source by evacuating him. Even if there's reason to think that counter-spies are closing in, there's also a temptation to milk him for one more delivery of documents or microfilm, one more morsel of information.

One defector-in-place who eventually was able to escape was Lieutenant Colonel Michal Goleniewski, of the Polish Intelligence Service. From 1958 to 1960, he passed information to the CIA, but then felt that he was taking too many risks and asked for evacuation. As his admission ticket, he gave information about KGB moles in Western organizations. He fingered George Blake in Britain, and Colonel Israel Beer, a Soviet spy, in Israel. However, there were those in the CIA who viewed him with suspicion, and who felt that he was giving out just enough valid information to establish credibility.[18]

Disparaging Defectors

If you're considering defecting to the other side, remember that you'll be burning your bridges behind you. Your government will try to paint you in as bad a light as possible, to discredit you with your own people. You'll be surprised to find yourself described as mentally ill, perverted, criminal, etc. This is, however, all part of the damage control procedure governments put into effect when a defection takes place.

When a citizen goes over to the other side, another set of standard and predictable reactions occur. The sudden appearance of a government employee at a press conference in the rival's capital is acutely embarrassing for his country of origin. Typically, the defector states that he was sick and tired of living under tyranny, oppression, capitalism, communism, imperialism, etc., and that he had come over to find freedom, equality, fair treatment, etc. He may or may not have his family with him.

His new host hails the defector as a clear-headed, freedom-loving person who made the right choice. His former country denounces him as a misfit, pervert, criminal, etc. Because the defector is now permanently beyond the reach of the security service, it becomes important, for public relations, to minimize his importance. Often, unless it's absolutely impossible to do so, the government will dismiss him as a low level official who had few secrets to betray, to avoid embarrassing the security service. This is an instance of a government using the cloak of secrecy to protect itself from its own people. Behind closed doors, of course, there will be an intensive damage-control effort.

Both logic and the scrutiny of defectors shows that they tend to be misfits, whether they are going from West to East or in the other direction. Logic states that they changed sides because they were unhappy where they were, while most of their fellow citizens remained to make the most of an imperfect world. If we look at the defectors whose histories are available to us, we can see that they went to the other side to leave behind difficult personal situations.

Guy Burgess and Donald Maclean, two British diplomats who had secretly spied for the Soviets for a decade or more, were both alcoholics and homosexuals whose careers were threatened by their vices. Both members of the English upper class, they obtained their jobs and were propped up by the "old boy" network when they faltered. British aristocrats are exceedingly tolerant of faults among their own, faults which they would ruthlessly punish in members of the lower classes.

Burgess was a notorious homosexual, during an era when homosexuality was not as tolerated as now. When drunk, he'd boast in explicit detail of his sexual contacts with North African boys, English working-class males, and anyone else in pants whom he could seduce.[19] Donald Maclean was bisexual, which may account for his several failed marriages. He also had a severe drinking problem, which caused a scandal when he was at the Cairo embassy, and resulted in his being shipped home. The precipitating factor in their escape across the English Channel, and then behind the Iron Curtain, was a tip-off from another member of the Cambridge spy ring that exposure was imminent.

In Moscow, Burgess kept up his heavy drinking, and died of cirrhosis of the liver while still in his 50s. Donald Maclean's latest marriage broke up, and his wife left him for Kim Philby, who by then had himself arrived in Moscow.

Talent-Spotting

Every embassy has a secret agent section, and many spy rings have talent scouts. Part of their job is to spot potential recruits. This often results in separation of functions. The Soviet United Nations Mission, for example, has its established procedure for recruiting and running spies. Soviet citizens without diplomatic immunity confine themselves to talent-spotting. The actual running of spies is the responsibility of the diplomats who, if caught, get "PNGed" out of the country forthwith.[20]

Sometimes, spotting and recruiting are very easy. A person may have relatives or friends in the other country, providing a link for exploitation. Other links are less direct, and require more exploitation.

The embassy guest book, which visitors are asked to sign, is one source of raw material. So are business contacts, if one country does a lot of trading with the other. Student exchange programs offer an entry as well, and friendships made during student visits may be promising enough for follow-up action. If one country publishes a magazine inside the other's territory, the subscription list can offer leads, as can letters to the editor.[21]

Soviet agents had talent scouts at Cambridge University during the 1920s and 1930s, looking for bright young men who appeared to be destined for high places. These worked in conjunction with a homosexual network, seeking out potential agents who would remain loyal to the Soviet Union for life. The technique was to get to know potential recruits personally, to explore their personalities and loyalties, and to discover if they had ideals subject to manipulation.

This was an outstandingly successful project, as it produced an entire generation of Soviet spies, all home-grown in the United Kingdom. They penetrated the Foreign Office, the Secret Intelligence Service, and the Security Service, protecting each other and laying false trails. Several defected to the Soviet Union, eventually dying of old age. Harold "Kim" Philby, the most successful one exposed, maintained that he'd betrayed his country because it was corrupt, and that the Soviet Union offered a better hope for humanity.

The Soviets have always taken the long view, and apparently still do. One case which came to light was the recruiting of Leakh N. Bhoge, a student from Guyana. Bhoge was a junior at Queens College, New York, when a Soviet UN employee named Zakharov approached him. Zakharov's mode of operation was to make the rounds of colleges in the New York area, seeking potential recruits for long-term operations. Bhoge was majoring in computers, and Zakharov's approach was to ask him for help in a research project. Bhoge photocopied unclassified material from the college library, a first step in providing services for Zakharov. The relationship continued, with Zakharov asking Bhoge to steal material from the library for him, and giving him help in finding employment. He told Bhoge to seek employment in artificial intelligence or an allied field, and offered to pay for graduate school if Bhoge wished to broaden his education. It appeared that the Soviets were prepared to stick with Bhoge for the long haul, hoping to develop him into a highly-placed agent in the defense industries.[22]

This particular plan misfired because Bhoge was working with the FBI, and informed them of Zakharov's activities. FBI Agents monitored the meetings between them, providing Bhoge with a micro-transmitter. The FBI found Bhoge a job with a firm making parts for a military contract, and arrested Zakharov when Bhoge passed classified documents to him on a subway platform.

Just as Tom Black had recruited Harry Gold during the 1930s, a Soviet national, Svetlana Ogorodnikov, was apparently a "contact agent," or talent scout, for the Soviet spy network on the United States' West Coast during 1973-1984. She recruited Richard Miller, an FBI Agent, and under her tutelage Miller handed over the FBI intelligence-gathering manual. This gave the Soviet intelligence service a good overview of FBI methods. However, Ogorodnikov over-reached herself in actually running Miller, because her lack of diplomatic immunity left her open to arrest and prosecution.[23]

There is an established procedure for seducing someone to spy for money. This is a variant of the salami-slicing technique, in which the control agent asks for more significant services as time goes by. If you get the assignment to develop the source, begin by inviting the potential informer out to dinner or the theater. If the subject is married, the invitation is for his wife, as well. If the potential defector invites you to his home, you will bring an expensive gift. Once the relationship is on a regular basis, it's time to move in on the potential recruit.

This stage begins with a request for a favor, something which the subject can easily provide in his line of work, and which is not illegal. It can be as innocent as information regarding the top officers in the company, or a copy of the internal telephone directory. Next comes a request for something more difficult to obtain, such as a copy of a contract his employer has received from the government. An easy explanation for why you want it is that a friend of yours is representing a rival company, and needs the information to adjust his company's bid on the next contract. You make cash payments for these services quickly and without fanfare, to make it clear to your subject that there's more money to earn, if he's willing to play along.

If you're the one being bribed, there's a real danger of getting carried away in opulence. Unless you're a level-headed type, you may be tempted to live the high life, which is often a fatal mistake. If you buy a Rolls-Royce or Maserati, you're advertising your affluence, and you'll definitely attract unwanted attention. Fellow employees will be scrutinizing you, enviously wondering the source of your new-found wealth. Plain, raw jealousy can lead to one or more unpleasant prospects:

1.   Someone reports you to the company security officer.

2.   Your neighbor or co-worker points you out to the FBI.

3.   Someone snitches to the IRS.

Don't under-estimate jealousy as a motive. An unfortunate personality trait some people have is the determination that if they can't have the golden ring, they'll spoil it for anyone who does.

Doubling-up

It's always worthwhile for a handler or spymaster to have two or more sources operating in the same area, or extracting the same information. Keeping agents from knowing about each other is important, for compartmenting and to retain their independence. This serves several important ends:

1.   Having two or more agents operating helps check one's performance against the other's. Spyhandlers know that some spies and traitors willingly sell false information, their motive being only money. They also know that some agents are not what they seem, and may be set-ups by

the target country's counter-espionage agency to pass false information.

2.   A second agent serves as a back-up in case the first agent gets caught.

3.   Agents rarely overlap exactly, and a second agent may have access to information unavailable to the first. The Israeli handlers had at least one more agent within the American intelligence establishment, who had enough familiarity with American intelligence documents that he was able to call them out by reference number. He, too, may have passed documents to the Israeli handlers, but one of his tasks certainly was listing documents which Pollard was to purloin.[24]

4.   Having more than one agent operating also serves as a source of information about the first agent's performance or status. A second agent can pass along impressions and gossip about everyone in his department, without knowing that one is also working for his handler.

Retirement

The fate of the spy who retires depends very much on whether he's a regular member of an espionage agency, or freelance. If you've sold your country's secrets to another power, and had the good sense to accept generous payment for them, you'll have accumulated a nest egg that will provide a lavish retirement.

If you're a bureaucrat, you'll have to make do on a government pension. It really doesn't matter how adventurous, valuable, or dangerous your work has been. Spies who survive to end their careers may find themselves disappointed, if they're working for their own country. A spy under diplomatic cover, or an "Illegal" sent abroad, is still a government employee, and government agencies are often cheap when it comes to pensions. You may collect special pay for hazardous duty, but that doesn't affect your pension. Even government espionage services that may spend outlandish amounts on special equipment, or may pay foreign citizens huge sums to betray their countries, are tight-fisted when it comes to their own.[25]

If you're a spy with access to a large expense account, it may be a wise precaution to divert some of the money into a personal retirement fund for yourself. Unless you know the terms of retirement for certain, and your government has a reputation for dealing fairly with its secret employees, you may find yourself out in the cold. The pension you finally get may be too small to allow you to live.[26]

In some cases, the espionage service can be very cheap. Klop Ustinov, father of the actor Peter Ustinov, worked for British Intelligence before, during, and after World War II. He received no pension, because he wasn't in it for the money, and did not take care to see that his superiors took care of him after retirement.[27] Peter Wright, who interviewed him on an intelligence-related project, concluded that MI-5 expected loyalty from its officers, but did not feel obliged to reciprocate.

Wright was very sensitive about this point, because he felt that MI-5 had treated him badly. He'd spent 15 years working for the British Admiralty, and when MI-5 had recruited him, he'd received a verbal assurance that his pension rights would be transferable. When it came time to retire, he found out that the verbal promise had evaporated, and that his status would be governed by written rules. These rules were not as generous as the verbal arrangement made with him years before. When he retired in January, 1976, his pension was significantly less than he'd felt was coming to him.[28] His bitterness over this may have been a factor in his writing his book, which embarrassed the British intelligence establishment.

Sources

1. *The FBI-KGB War*, Robert J. Lamphere, NY, Berkeley Books, 1987, p. 33.

2. *Merchants of Treason*, Thomas B. Allen and Norman Polmar, NY, Dell Books, 1988, p. 52.

3. *FBI-KGB War*, p. 171.

4. *Ibid.*, pp. 181-185.

5. *Ibid.*, p. 192.

6. *Spyclopedia*, Richard Deacon, NY, Silver Arrow Books, 1988, pp. 271-272.

7. *Merchants of Treason*, pp. 372-377.

8. *Mask of Treachery*, John Costello, NY, Warner Books, 1988, p. 170.

9. *Spyclopedia*, pp. 296-297.

10. *The Book of Lies*, M. Hirsh Goldberg, NY, Morrow and Company, 1990, pp. 232-233.

11. *New York Times*, May 26, 1988.

12. *The Spy Who Got Away*, David Wise, NY, Avon Books, 1988, p. 15.

13. *Spyclopedia*, pp. 268-269.

14. *Ibid.*, pp. 290-291.

15. *The Circus*, Nigel West, NY, Stein and Day, 1982, pp. 36 and 39.

16. *Mask of Treachery*, p. 471.

17. *Spyclopedia*, pp. 202-203.

18. *Ibid.*, pp. 299-300.

19. *Mask of Treachery*, p. 193.

20. *Merchants of Treason*, p. 211.

21. The U.S.S.R. publishes a magazine called *Soviet Life* in the United States. The American Embassy in Moscow publishes *Amerika*, under reciprocal agreement.

22. *Merchants of Treason*, pp. 211- 213.

23. *Ibid.*, pp. 267-272.

24. *Territory of Lies*, Wolf Blitzer, NY, Harper Paperbacks, 1989, p. 296. Pollard told his American interrogators that his handler had instructed him to obtain certain documents, which he identified by code number and title, something he could not have known without at least one more source within American intelligence.

25. *Handbook for Spies*, p. 7.

26. *Ibid.*, pp. 101-103.

27. *Spycatcher*, Peter Wright, NY, Dell Books, 1987, pp. 87-88.

28. *Ibid.*, p. 462.

5

Infiltration

~~~~~~

One way of getting spies into another country is by infiltrating. This can be by several means. One long-standing technique is open infiltration, through diplomatic channels. Another is illegal infiltration.

The Diplomatic Agent

As we've already seen, every embassy, consulate, or diplomatic mission has its spy. He may hold a title such as "Commercial Attache" or "Passport Control Officer." Often, an embassy or consulate has more than one secret operative under diplomatic cover. A chauffeur or cook may be a top-ranking secret agent, despite his lowly official title. Low rank is a protection against counter-espionage surveillance. The FBI is more likely to keep tabs on a second secretary than a maid.

The advantage of having diplomatic cover is immunity from prosecution. The Vienna Convention of 1815 formally established "diplomatic immunity," as this privileged status was necessary to prevent intimidation or harassment of legitimate diplomats during difficult periods. Diplomatic immunity has also been abused. A diplomat can hold meetings with the host country's traitors, secure in the knowledge that, if caught, he'll be on the next airplane out of the country, while his contact will face the firing squad. The reason is that, under the Vienna Convention, a diplomat who is a bad guest is immune to arrest, but subject to being declared "persona non grata," a polite diplomatic term for "Adios M— F—." This can happen as a result of too many traffic violations, an adulterous affair, or even felonious conduct. One who receives "persona non grata," or is "PNGed" (pronounced "PINGED"), has to leave as soon as possible, and is henceforth unwelcome in that country.

The negative aspects the diplomatic spy must endure are the limitations on movement, and the surveillance. The host country may declare certain areas off limits for the diplomat from a suspect or unfriendly country. The restriction may be quite severe, such as limiting the diplomats' travel to within 25 miles of the embassy or consulate.

Surveillance is a constant hassle. The Federal Bureau of Investigation's New York field office has over 1,000 agents, because of the large number of diplomats at the United Nations. Western diplomats in Moscow have complained about oppressive KGB surveillance.

The "illegal" agent can operate free of surveillance, as long as he doesn't fall under suspicion. However, he has no protection if the target country's counter-spies find him. He does have certain advantages, which we can examine now.

The Illegal Agent

This is the person who slips into the country under a false identity. His job is usually not to infiltrate into a sensitive position, but to manage agents who are already passing information. The reason is that modern security checks make it very difficult to fabricate a persona to slip through the security screen. Anyone applying for sensitive employment must go through a process known as a "security clearance," during which investigators check the person's background and interview neighbors, friends, relatives, and former employers.

In countries with relatively lax security, such as most of the Western countries, it's relatively easy to slip agents in over the border and to have them set up residence. American borders are very porous, as evidenced by the heavy traffic in both illegal immigrants and drugs. The United States has a large foreign population, and an accent isn't cause for suspicion.

The illegal agent cannot infiltrate into a high-security position, but he can be a handler for other agents. On a lower level, he can be a courier, whose only task is to convey material from one person or point to another. He may even operate a mail drop or a dead drop, for receipt of materials.

To infiltrate an agent into a country with strict border controls requires other means. An agent may infiltrate with false papers, but if he has a certain amount of clandestine equipment, such as a radio transceiver, he may be infiltrated by air. This might be by parachute drop, as the British and American services tried against Albania during the late 1940s, or it may be by sending a totally "sanitized" aircraft to make an illicit landing in enemy territory to drop off the agents. This happened against the Soviet Union during the early 1950s. There had been some information leaks that the Soviet Air Defense Force was preparing a vast network of radar sites and interceptor airfields in the North, responding to the threat of attack by the U.S. Strategic Air Command. The CIA sent two-man teams by seaplane into the North Russian wilderness to observe and report back.[1]

If you're a member of such an infiltration team, you're betting your freedom, and maybe even your life, that your control officer is competent. Remember, you're going in on your own: he's not sharing the risks with you. Of course, he'll tell you that a team of experts have gone over every aspect of your mission, and that they've got every contingency figured to assure your safety. He wouldn't tell you anything else, because he wants your morale and confidence in him to be high.

If you're going in by air, you'd better hope that the control officer and your pilot planned the route to avoid the target country's radar. Otherwise, you might meet unwelcome company on the way in, and receive a hot rocket enema in mid-air.

If you're to mix with the local population, your papers had better be in order. This is where much can go wrong. You might have a travel permit signed by "Colonel Ivanov," but on the date the permit was allegedly issued, Ivanov had not yet taken his post, and "Major Gromov" was in charge. This is the type of small detail that can betray you. As we'll see later, sometimes the oversight is deliberate.

What about communication? Is your radio really as good as you've been assured it is? Does it really transmit on such a tight beam that enemy direction-finding stations can't pick it up? Your antenna system may have prominent side-lobes, which give away the location to anyone within your radius. If it's a "squirt radio," is transmission time really too short for enemy direction-finders to triangulate?

During World War II, both sides parachuted infiltration agents into enemy controlled territory. Most had short careers, because of inadequate preparation, bad luck, and the skill of the counter-espionage agencies. Secret services on both sides relied on large numbers of agents, secretly acknowledging the inadequate training and preparation they provided for their agents, but calculating that the enemy couldn't catch them all.

William Casey, later to become the head of the CIA, spent part of his World War II career in the OSS section that parachuted agents into Germany. The agents made tiny contributions, in reality, and Casey never expected much from them. His section would equip an agent with a radio, drop him behind the lines, and hope that the agent would survive and make contact.[2]

The Sleeper Agent

The "sleeper" is a deep-cover agent who takes up residence in the target country and does nothing until "activated." One sleeper was Emil Koedel, a German-born agent for the Abwehr who had served in the U.S. Army during World War I, then had returned to Germany in 1935 to serve in its espionage service. He returned to New York, where he lived and worked, and waited for a call to action. In 1939, he received a letter activating him, and he began spying in his low-key way. He joined the U.S. Ordnance Association, and through his membership contacts, obtained military information to relay to the fatherland.[3]

There are several reasons for setting up a network of sleepers. One is that the main vulnerability of espionage agents is their communications.[4] Meets, letters, drops, and radio signals are all open to interception or observation. Even a "dubok," or dead drop, can be under observation. If an agent's immediate services aren't essential, it's better to let him remain in place, without contact, until he's needed.

Another reason is to keep him as a reserve, in case an operational agent becomes inactivated. Counter-espionage police may arrest an agent, or he may fall ill or die in a traffic accident. A back-up ensures continuity.

A sleeper agent may be a safe house operator, who simply maintains the premises year after year. He may never be needed, but a recognition signal may come someday, alerting him to expect guests. The signal may be a letter or postcard, or it may be something left in a dead drop which the sleeper "services" regularly.

Yet another reason is contingency. A sleeper may perform a function that is unnecessary unless war comes. For example, one unverified rumor is that British Intelligence had placed a sleeper agent in one of Germany's main ports to observe the naval base. During peacetime, this was not a crucial function, but once World War II began, the movements of German naval vessels was vital information. After World War II, when American planners feared a Soviet surprise attack, the CIA allegedly established surveillance agents near Russian bomber bases. These agents would activate only if they saw large numbers of bombers taking off, in which case they would radio their controls that an attack was on the way.

The Fake Refugee

After World War II, various Eastern Bloc intelligence agencies slipped thousands of agents across the line into Western countries as refugees or exiles. Some attained high posts within Western governments. The West German government was especially vulnerable to this sort of infiltration, and several persons from East Germany were able to infiltrate sensitive agencies and relay information back to the East.

In 1963, three East German infiltrators, Hans Clemens, Heinz Felfe, and Erwin Tiebel, were arrested and tried. These had been employed in various sensitive West German intelligence and security posts, while they passed classified materials to their controls in the East. Another East German agent, Gunther Guillaume, worked in the office of West German Chancellor Willy Brandt as a confidential assistant. He took the opportunity to relay confidential information to the East German espionage agency until his arrest in April, 1974.[5]

Larry Wu-Tai Chin was a Chinese infiltrator who had first begun working for the United States in 1948, during China's civil war, as a translator. His career spanned over three decades, as he moved from the U.S. Army Liaison Office in Foochow to the CIA's translation and monitoring service. Although he never attained a high rank within the CIA, over the years he was able to pass a lot of valuable information simply because he was there. He borrowed documents for photocopying, returning them without detection. In fact, American counter-spies didn't arrest him until after he'd retired from the CIA.

Infiltration into a hostile country can be difficult or almost impossible. It's much easier if you're spying on an ally. Many nations do exactly this, and we'll look at some examples next.

Sources

1. *The Secret Team*, L. Fletcher Prouty, NY, Ballantine Books, 1974, pp. 177-188.

2. *Spying For America*, Nathan Miller, NY, Dell Books, 1989, p. 343.

3. *Nazi Spies in America*, William Breuer, NY, St. Martin's Press, 1989, pp. 136-139.

4. *Catching Spies*, H.H.A. Cooper and Lawrence J. Redlinger, NY, Bantam Books, 1990, pp. 112-116.

5. *KGB/CIA Intelligence and Counter-intelligence Operations*, Celina Bledowska and Jonathan Bloch, NY, Bison Books, 1987, p. 80.

6
Spying
On
Allies

∞∞∞∞∞∞∞∞∞∞∞∞∞∞∞∞∞∞∞∞∞∞∞∞∞∞∞∞∞∞

One of the most embarrassing secrets of the espionage trade is that countries often spy upon their allies, as well as upon enemies and rivals. This is because the plans and activities of allies can be as worrisome as those of enemies, in certain circumstances. Recent history provides many examples which have come to light, and no doubt there are many more which remain secret.

During World War II, for example, the Western Allies did not fully trust the Soviets, and worried that Stalin might come to a peace agreement with Hitler. Likewise, Stalin did not trust his Western allies. He suspected that they were holding off on the "second front" he was demanding, in the hope that Germany and Russia would destroy each other. This would allow Britain and the United States to walk in and pick up the pieces. Articles appearing in the American press, advocating exactly this policy, were not reassuring. The Soviets could not understand that, with a free press, it's possible to publish opinions that contradict government policy, even during wartime.

The Germans had problems with Italy, because they knew that Italy was not holding up its end in the war effort, and Mussolini's rule was shaky. Indeed, in 1943, Mussolini lost his job as leader of Italy, and under Marshall Badoglio, the Italian Government signed a separate peace with the Allies.

The Italians themselves, while still allies with Germany, undertook to spy upon at least one nation with which Italy and Germany were still at peace. The Italian Secret Service carried out a "black bag job" on the U.S. Embassy to steal the diplomatic code. Italian officers did not actually break into the embassy, because two Italian nationals working as indigenous civilian employees were also working for Italian Military Intelligence. They simply copied the code during their regular hours at the embassy. The effects were far-reaching, as being able to read American diplomatic traffic allowed the Italians to monitor the detailed messages that Colonel Bonner Fellers, American military attache, was sending home from Cairo. Fellers gave Washington full information regarding British military dispositions in the war in North Africa, and this information helped General Rommel deploy his limited forces more effectively.[1]

During World War II, Soviet Russian agents ran several espionage rings in the United States and Great Britain, directed against their wartime allies. The official Russian mission in New York, for example, housed Anatoly Yakovlev, an NKVD officer who was case officer for the Rosenberg spy ring. Another Soviet spy ring centered around the Russian Embassy in Ottawa, Canada, and this was the one revealed by Igor Gouzenko, who defected to the Canadians in 1945.

Soviet espionage against the United States actually began in the 1920s, and concentrated on industrial processes needed to modernize Russian industry. Philip Jacob Jaffe, born in the Ukraine, became a naturalized American citizen in 1923, and went on to establish a subversive organization. During the 1930s, the "Ware Ring" started operation in the United States. Six of its members worked for the U. S Government's Agricultural Adjustment Administration: Alger Hiss, Lee Pressman, John Abt, Nathan Witt, Nathaniel Weyl, and Charles Kramer. Hiss later attained a high position in the State department. In the Treasury Department, Soviet infiltrators were: Harry Dexter White, Frank Coe, Harold Glasser, Victor Perlo, Irving Kaplan, Sol Adler, Abraham George Silverman, and William Ullman. Most of these, as previously pointed out, were of Jewish backgrounds.

Britain spied upon France. After World War II, the British Security Service had developed a technical surveillance method of reading the impulses from electro-mechanical rotor cipher machines, beginning with those used by the Egyptian Embassy. They soon moved on to others, among them the French Embassy in London. Britain's Government Communications Headquarters routinely intercepts telephone and teletype traffic from each embassy in London, and MI-5 took advantage of this to crack the French rotor machine.[2]

The American National Security Agency has what is probably the largest code-cracking system in the world. The NSA regularly intercepts and decodes the messages of friend and foe alike. This is what made the defections of Martin and Mitchell, and their subsequent press conference in Moscow, so embarrassing for the United States. A cooperative effort by the U.S. Navy and NSA has resulted in a small fleet of intelligence ships, performing exactly the same functions as the Russian trawlers that regularly appear off the American coast. The Liberty, attacked by Israel in 1967, was one of these, designed to intercept radio traffic from friendly and unfriendly sources.

Israel ran spies against the United States, and at least one of these came to light, in the "Pollard Affair." The United States has been Israel's biggest benefactor since the Jewish state began in 1948, sending both financial and military aid each year. The amount of aid has been so great, lately averaging 3.5 billion per year, that it's safe to say that without the United States there would be no Israel today. Nevertheless, the thinking in espionage agencies is very unsentimental, and "gratitude" is not part of the vocabulary.

Unknown to many people in the Israeli Government, and even within the Mossad, there is a special section known as "Al" which conducts espionage on American soil. This unit has infiltrated American intelligence sections concerned with Middle East information, and it relays information to Israel.[3] The unit also strives to obtain political information, such as which legislators are planning to vote on an issue important to Israel, and to this end will even recruit a Jewish member of a Congressman's staff to pass papers and information to it. Industrial espionage is also part of the picture, because Israeli Intelligence also supports Israeli business in its efforts to win contracts, and industrial secrets can provide a competitive edge.

There are several motives for spying upon an ally:

One is to confirm that what the allied government is telling you is true, and that it's living up to agreements with you.

Another is to monitor any changes in the other government's policy. Allies don't always remain allies, and it helps to have early warning of a change in alignment.

Another reason is that even staunch allies often find that their policies and interests don't coincide 100%. An example is Britain's continuing to trade with the People's Republic of China, even during the Korean War. A spy can help uncover hidden policies and interests.

Some nations, although nominally allies, have a history of treachery so prominent that it's foolish to trust them. Many such examples exist in the Mid-East. A strong espionage effort can provide early warning of impending treachery and allow your country to avoid getting hurt.

Another motive is to obtain secret information which you don't have the resources to get for yourself. An example of this is satellite photos of Middle Eastern countries, which Jonathan Pollard handed over to the Israelis. The Soviet effort to obtain nuclear bomb data from the Allied Powers during World War II was to keep its own scientists abreast of latest developments. Although the Russians, thanks to Peter Kapitza, were not newcomers to nuclear physics, they wanted to have up-to-date information on what the United States, Britain, and Canada were developing for military use.

Yet another reason is to give you an edge in the exchange of secret information. Allies regularly exchange secret intelligence, but often on a quid pro quo basis. Your ally will provide you with material, provided you make it worthwhile, and hand over an equal amount of material. If you're getting information under the table, you can keep more to yourself in open exchanges. One cynical Israeli agent described his relationship with his American counterparts thus: "When I am sitting with my friend, he is not sitting with his friend."[4]

There are several reasons for allies to withhold information from each other, even though they may have a regular program of information exchange:

Information is a bargaining chip. A nation can use it to obtain information from another's intelligence service, or withhold it to pressure for a change in policy.

Revealing information may disclose too much about its origin. A foreign intelligence analyst may be able to deduce the source from the nature of the information. This is why certain intelligence documents are stamped "NOFOR" or equivalent, which means "No foreign dissemination." Documents intended for release to an ally often have deletions, to protect agents and other sources. The Israelis, for example, did not reveal to the American government that the Soviets were reading its naval codes, in order to protect a highly-placed Israeli agent within the Soviet military.

The allied government itself may harbor spies, and they may pass secret documents or information to an enemy.

The ally may also, despite a pledge to keep all information within its borders, barter the released information in an exchange with the intelligence service of a third country, which may not be friendly to the country of origin. This sort of cynical double-dealing happens, the only limits being the generosity of the government supplying the information, and the ethics of the government receiving it.

Sabotage Against Allies

In certain situations, a country may put aside its ethics and conduct sabotage operations against its friends for expediency. One such operation culminated in the "Lavon Affair," in Israel. During the early 1950s the Israelis found the U.S. government's friendliness towards Egypt disturbing. The Eisenhower Administration saw Nasser's Egypt as an anti-communist ally in the Middle East, but to the Israelis, Egypt was an enemy, and they wanted to discourage American aid at all costs. The Israelis cooked up a plan to use members of their espionage ring in Egypt, fortified by members of a special army sabotage unit, to blow up British and American installations in Egypt. The plan was to make it appear that Egyptian fundamentalists were responsible. There was a fair amount of damage done, but the Egyptian security service caught many of those responsible, and several died on the gallows.[5]

Sources

1. *Secret Warfare, The Battle of Codes and Ciphers*, Bruce Norman, NY, Dorset Press, 1973, pp. 123-124.

2. *Spycatcher*, Peter Wright, NY, Dell Books, 1987, pp. 138-141.

3. *By Way of Deception*, Victor Ostrovsky, NY, St. Martin's Press, 1990, pp. 269-272.

4. *Ibid.*, pp. 85-86.

5. *The Mossad*, Dennis Eisenberg, Uri Dan, and Eli Landau, NY, Paddington Press, 1978, pp. 77-81.

7

Evacuation

〰〰〰〰〰〰〰〰〰〰〰〰〰〰〰〰〰〰〰〰〰〰〰〰〰

Any spy operating in enemy territory has to worry about what can happen upon discovery. It's part of the control agent's job to reassure him that he probably won't be discovered, but that if he is, there is a plan to get him to safety. Sometimes, there's an emergency number to call. In other instances, the spy has to depend upon his own resources to implement the escape plan.

The Rosenberg spy ring was allegedly well-prepared for escape if discovered. David and Ruth Greenglass, Julius's in-laws, told how Julius had stated that plans existed for them to flee to Mexico, and thence to Russia. Julius Rosenberg went so far as to give Greenglass a thousand dollars in get-away money.[1] However, Ruth Greenglass was in the hospital at the time, and FBI Agents were close-tailing David, which aborted this plan. The Rosenbergs also were unable to escape, as FBI Agents arrested them before they could flee.

Another spy in the ring, Joel Barr, was in Paris at the time of the arrests, and he vanished about June 16, 1950. Another member of the ring, Morton Sobell, took his wife and children with him to Mexico City, on June 22, 1950. Yet another, Alfred Sarant, slipped out from under FBI surveillance on August 4, and made his way with his mistress by car to the American Southwest, from which they crossed into Mexico. The FBI did get Sobell back, however, by arrangement with the Mexican security police. On the evening of August 16, Mexican security agents arrested Sobell, and took his family into informal but tight custody. Two days later, the Mexicans handed Sobell over to FBI Agents at the border town of Laredo, Texas, and escorted his family across into the United States.[2]

Morris and Lona Cohen, hard-core Soviet agents, disappeared during the Rosenberg investigation. Their connection with the Rosenbergs was unclear, because Julius and Ethel went to their deaths without spilling their guts. The Cohens' work for their Soviet masters didn't end with their evacuation from America, as they turned up in England in 1961. When British counterspies broke the "Portland Spy Case," they raided and searched the home of a couple named Peter and Helen Kroger, who had papers showing them to be New Zealanders. The search disclosed short-wave transmitters, microdot equipment, a one-time code pad, and other espionage materials. A fingerprint check showed that the Krogers were actually the Cohens. In 1969, the British Government traded the Kroger/Cohens for Gerald Brooke, a British national who had been in Soviet custody.[3]

A British businessman named Greville Wynne played a role in an escape plan that went sour. Colonel Oleg Penkovsky, a Soviet defector-in-place, had been providing information to both the British and American espionage organizations for several years. Penkovsky was a GRU officer who had access to high-level information, and who used a variety of methods to hand it over. In one case, he passed microfilms to the wife of a British secret service agent operating under diplomatic cover in Moscow. The KGB began closing in on Penkovsky, tipped off by a mole in either the British or American espionage establishments. The escape plan was for Wynne to take a house trailer rigged as a traveling trade exhibit with him on one of his trips behind the iron curtain. The trailer had a secret compartment large enough to hide a person. The KGB found out about the escape plan, and arrested Wynne, to exchange him for Gordon Lonsdale in 1964. Penkovsky never escaped, although his eventual fate is uncertain. Some sources claim that he was tried and shot, while others state that the KGB had exposed and turned him, using him as a conduit for feeding false information to the West.

One reason for compartmenting information is to prevent the agent from knowing how often evacuation plans fail. Another is that evacuation may not be part of the larger plan. The control agent may decide to sacrifice one of his agents to protect another. The decision regarding whom to sacrifice and whom to protect depends not upon loyalty, but on the value of the information each agent can provide.

If, for example, a control agent has two agents in the target country's ministry of defense, one a colonel and the other a clerk, it's obvious that the colonel probably can provide more and better information than the clerk. If counter-espionage officers become suspicious, and begin looking for a "leak," both are in danger. If it's possible to make the clerk appear to have been pilfering all of the information, the handler may decide to let him go. He may even bring about his discovery, by asking him to take greater risks, or by planting a fake defector to expose him.

Sources

1. *The FBI-KGB War*, Robert J. Lamphere, NY, Berkeley Books, 1987, p. 192.

2. *Ibid.*, pp. 195-209.

3. *Spyclopedia*, Richard Deacon, NY, Silver Arrow Books, 1988, p. 281.

8

The
Lethal
Pill

According to many accounts, control officers provide their agents with "L-Pills" to kill themselves in case
of capture. In real life, contrary to fictional accounts,
this is rare. The reason is that most people don't have
the guts to kill themselves, even when faced with a
threat they might consider worse than death. Francis
Gary Powers, the U-2 pilot, had a poisoned needle with
him when his aircraft was shot down over the Soviet
Union in 1960. The poisoned needle was not a dummy,
as the Soviets found out by testing it upon an animal.
Powers also had a pistol and a knife, both of which
would have served for suicide. He used none of these,
and faced Soviet interrogation as a result. Fortunately

for Powers, his interrogation was strictly low-key, without torture.

The reason for the mild treatment given Powers is open to speculation. One obvious possibility is that the Soviets planned a show trial from the start, and did not want to have the world's media show a man who had the marks of torture all over his body. Another is that the KGB had long abandoned physical torture, despite recent propaganda, and now relied upon verbal and psychological interrogation. A third possibility is that Powers' interrogator correctly assessed him as a soft case, who lacked the backbone to resist. This is the most likely prospect, as Powers' behavior during the trial was that of a man who fully cooperated with his captors. His attitude was totally abject as he confessed his acts, and threw himself on the mercy of the court. His sentence was ten years, but in fact he got out in 18 months, in an exchange for Colonel Rudolf Abel.

Jonathan Jay Pollard, the American intelligence analyst who passed classified documents to Israel during 1984 and 1985, later stated that if his handlers had issued him a pill it probably would have been a placebo.[1]

There are no documented cases, but circumstantial evidence suggests that, in some instances, this might be true. Spymasters who want one of their agents caught, for disinformation purposes, do what they can to assure capture. They may issue defective false documents that betray the agent at first inspection, or even leak the word to the other side's counter-espionage police through a double agent. A genuine lethal pill would negate the entire effort.

Some captured spies succeed in killing themselves, even during captivity. One such was Max Benet, member of an Israeli spy and sabotage ring in Egypt, whom counter-spies captured in 1954. On December 21, 1954, he cut the blood vessels in his wrists and bled to death in his cell.[2]

The reason for his suicide may appear obvious, depending on which version we accept. However, Benet left no suicide note, and we can only speculate upon his motive. The motive that reflects best on him is that he killed himself to avoid being forced to give information to his interrogators. A less creditable one is that he did it to avoid torture. At the time, Egyptian police interrogators used physical torture routinely, and any question-and-answer session would become very rigorous. Benet was one of the leading figures of this particular spy ring, and the Egyptians knew it. This would focus their efforts on him, and he knew that they would squeeze him as much as possible.

Larry Wu-Tai Chin, convicted agent for the Chinese, asphyxiated himself with a plastic bag over his head while in jail awaiting sentencing in 1985. As he left no note, it's unclear exactly why he did it, but his age, and the prospect of a life sentence, were probably important.[3]

Today's technology of death allows a variety of pills and devices. Shellfish toxin, for example, is quick-acting, so that timely medical treatment is unlikely. The old standby, potassium cyanide, is as effective today as ever, and one way to use it is by keeping a capsule in a hollow tooth. Although Heinrich Himmler, Germany's S.S. Chief, wasn't a spy, he kept a cyanide capsule in a hollow tooth because he feared capture. Indeed, shortly after British troops captured him in 1945, he killed himself by crushing the capsule between his teeth. Hermann Goering, German Air Force Chief, avoided the hangman by swallowing cyanide after his trial and conviction.

Another category of drugs used in espionage is powerful sedatives and tranquilizers. When the Soviets discovered that Konstantin Volkov wanted to go over to the British, they faced the problem of getting him and his wife out of Turkey and back on Soviet soil. They did this by drugging them heavily, strapping them to stretchers, and flying them out of the country. Using drugs for control of involuntary subjects is a standard technique today.

The Israeli agents who abducted Adolf Eichmann and spirited him out of Argentina injected him with a powerful tranquilizer for the trip through Buenos Aires to the airport, where they bundled him aboard a special El-Al flight. Egyptian agents in Rome tried to smuggle a captured Israeli agent out of Italy and back to Cairo by drugging him, and putting him in a special trunk.

When it's necessary to liquidate someone on the spot, there's an array of deadly drugs and delivery systems available. Many espionage agencies have teams of specialists in covert assassination.

Sources

1. *Territory of Lies*, Wolf Blitzer, NY, Harper Paperbacks, 1989, p. 179.

2. *Decline of Honor*, Avri El-Ad, Chicago, Henry Regnery Company, 1976, p. 172.

3. *Merchants of Treason*, Thomas B. Allen and Norman Polmar, NY, Dell Books, 1988, p. 377.

9

Security

〰〰〰〰〰〰〰〰〰〰〰〰〰〰〰〰〰〰〰〰〰〰〰〰〰

There are two categories of counter-measures against spying. One is passive. The other is active. Passive measures fall under "security," which corresponds to building fences and keeping doors locked. "Counter-espionage" covers active measures, which we'll discuss in the next chapter. Let's first take a good look at security, because that's where it begins.

Security works both ways: to protect your secrets, and to deny an adversary knowledge of how deeply you've compromised his. An effective security program also makes it easier to trace the path of an information leak, and to estimate how much damage a penetration has done.

Security covers several aspects: physical security, personnel security, information control, and document control. Physical security is a system of walls, fences, alarms, patrols, safe rooms, and locks to deny physical access to unauthorized persons. Every sensitive government office and every defense contractor is required to employ some physical security safeguards. This is called "access control," and in theory denies easy access to unauthorized persons. The problem with all physical security is that it doesn't help much against authorized persons who decide to leak information.

Personnel Security

Personnel security means investigating each person before granting access to classified information. This can include evaluating an application, routine checks of selected items, background checks, and intensive investigation for the highest clearances. Clearances generally correspond to security levels, which range from "Confidential" to "Top Secret" and beyond. There are special classifications for specially protected information. Some are the "Q-Clearance" for nuclear weapon information, and the "Crypto" clearance for code and cipher information. There are other categories where even the clearance term is classified.

An important aspect of personnel security is screening out high-risk types, which experience has shown are less trustworthy than others. The obvious risks are those with criminal records, or a drug or alcohol problem. Another high-risk type is the homosexual, because of his vulnerability to blackmail. Even in today's atmosphere of "gay pride" and openness about sexual orientation, the risk exists. It may be permissible, and even trendy, to declare one's sexual preference openly in certain occupations, such as cosmetics, fashion, and entertainment, but in government employ it's typically forbidden. Despite a few recent court decisions, the armed forces will not knowingly accept a homosexual recruit, nor will most law enforcement agencies. Agencies involved in national security likewise frown upon sexual deviates of any sort, and anyone with such propensities risks his career if he admits them.

This policy isn't, as "gay rights" advocates may charge, the result of "homophobia." It's simply avoidance of any sort of deviant behavior which may subject the person to blackmail. A child molester, for example, is liable to prosecution whether the child is male or female. A spy recruiter who uncovers this information has powerful leverage to coerce the molester into betraying his country. Someone with a taste for whips and chains, or leather fetishism, is also vulnerable to blackmail. In most Western countries, conduct between consenting adults behind closed doors is tolerated, but a government employee still might not want photographs of himself bound in chains during a sexual act to be mailed to his supervisor. This is true even in countries which have supposedly more liberal attitudes towards sexual perversion than the United States.

The British experience shows that there was an underground ring of homosexuals spying for Soviet

Russia from the late 1920s to the 1960s, and perhaps beyond. This circle, although it had a few heterosexual members, revolved mainly around some who were notorious homosexuals. These included Anthony Blunt, David Maclean, and even tangentially included one or two members of the Royal family, although not all homosexual members spied for Russia.[1]

Other risk factors are loyalties to foreign powers, including allies. Relatives abroad, for example, may be liabilities. One American with three sons living in Israel found his security clearance revoked.[2] The Pollard affair threw the question of American-Israeli dual loyalties into focus, and American security officials are taking a closer look at Jews in sensitive positions.

Hard experience has shown that people apparently loyal can "turn," and security clearances are not for life. Depending on the government and the level of clearance, there's a regular program of renewing or updating every cleared person's security check. Security agents reinterview relatives, friends, neighbors, fellow employees, and others who know the subject, to ascertain if there's been any significant development. A marriage or divorce may be significant, especially marriage to a foreign national. A change in drinking habits is also a danger signal, as is use of drugs. Gambling debts can accumulate, tempting the person with a security clearance to sell his country's secrets for cash. Foreign travel may be significant, as handlers prefer to meet deep-cover agents in foreign countries. Certain countries known to be safe havens for foreign intelligence services are alert signs. Austria has long been receptive to Soviet Bloc agents, for example, and the Soviet Embassy in Mexico City is a center for activity centered upon the United States.

A taste for the high life is also a danger signal. Anyone with "champagne tastes and a beer budget" may be looking for another source of income, even if it's illegal.

Information Security

Information control is a system of deciding what information is safe to release, and what items require close guard. It's impossible to protect every scrap of information, nor is it necessary. Among items of information publicly known are military budgets, numbers of personnel, and locations of bases. Secret items are war plans, specific budget items, amounts of supplies dedicated to a particular project, codes and ciphers, and information-gathering capabilities.

Protecting information also involves compartmenting, a system of telling each employee or agent only what he "needs to know" to do his job. The reason for this policy is simple and obvious; you can't reveal what you don't know. An engineer or draftsman involved with the design of a new weapon knows only what he needs to know to complete his job. Allowing him access to secret information about other weapons, or other topics unrelated to his function, would be very dangerous. If one of your people betrays you, you don't want him giving away the whole store.

Security also applies to spy rings. The spymaster or control agent tells each member of his ring only what he needs to know. Capture is an ever-present danger, and a captured agent can reveal only what he knows. If the ring is properly compartmented, he'll be able to lead counter-spies to only one or two other members. In some cases, with a system of dead drops, he may not be able to do even that.

There are abuses in classification of information. Secret services often use "security" to withhold knowledge of their blunders and failures from the people who pay their salaries. Government leaders who aren't "cleared" never learn exactly why an operation went wrong, or even that it did. The public is often the last to know, as espionage and security executives bury their unnecessary casualties under a layer of secrecy.

At times, normal secrecy serves to conceal slovenly performance. Richard Miller, the FBI agent who worked in the counter-intelligence section in Los Angeles, provides an example. His former supervisors in the FBI described him as "slovenly," and careless in safeguarding government materials and in carrying out his duties. Obviously, they have to answer for keeping such an unsuitable person in a sensitive position, but because of institutionalized secrecy, they may never have to account for their oversight.[3]

Another problem with Miller was the "Mormon Mafia," a group of FBI Agents in the Los Angeles field office. There were allegations that, in that office, the Mormons practiced favoritism, as the top executives, including the Special Agent in Charge, were Mormons. There had even been a complaint made to the Equal Opportunity Employment Commission by an agent who was not Mormon.[4]

Document Security

Document control is strict surveillance and tracing of each secret document. Certain rules always apply. There is a limit on access to documents, restricted to those who are both cleared, and who have a "need to know." Nobody is allowed to remove documents from controlled facilities, especially not to take home. Every document has a serial number, and each person taking it for study must sign for it. Copying of secret documents without special authorization is forbidden. All obsolete documents, or those no longer needed, go into special disposal containers. Some go through shredders, others are burned, and highly sensitive documents go through both shredding and incineration.

This system allows tracing everyone who had access to a particular document, and narrowing the suspect list when something is missing or found to be in enemy hands. A further method allows cutting the suspect list to very few people. If the document is text, not a drawing, computer-generated text allows making each copy individual. A special computer program can make each copy different, in several inconspicuous ways. Punctuation can be different, as can certain terms. The number of words on each page can vary, as can line width and spacing. Specific tangential information can be varied. For example, a document may list the entire budget as $54,415,630.87 and another copy will list the "cents" column as 86 cents. These differences allow tracing a document, even if photocopied or retyped.

The War Plan

Another aspect of security planning is the war contingency plan. Competent security agencies maintain an arrest list of security risks to round up and intern upon the outbreak of war. The list can include enemy aliens, members of organizations sympathetic to an enemy country or a hostile ideology, friends and relatives of these suspicious persons, and suspected security risks against whom there is insufficient evidence for prosecution.

The security agency, usually in collaboration with the army, has a number of internment camps prepared for activation at the outset of war. Army reservists, rather than front-line troops, staff these camps. There is a stack of emergency arrest or detention warrants already in place at each security office in the country, and plans to enlist local and military police to carry out arrests. Warrants are filled out on each prospective detainee, with only the date left blank. There are also blank warrants for last-minute additions. Security officers, police, and troops are likely to work round the clock, until all persons on the lists are in custody.

Another crucial aspect of wartime security is control of access to sensitive areas. Military bases will be closed to all civilians other than those employed there. Important facilities, such as power plants, industrial plants, and transportation centers, will acquire teams of guards to prevent sabotage. Certain areas, such as frontier zones, may be off-limits to any but residents, and in extreme cases it may become necessary to evacuate residents to give the military a free hand. It may also become necessary to create a system of travel permits, to control traffic, and avoid overcrowding trains and planes.

Security officers also intensify surveillance of points of entry, to control traffic in and out of the country. They may even deny entry or exit to anyone without a special permit. In wartime, diplomatic personnel can theoretically travel freely, but in practice there are restrictions, and secret agents intercept and examine diplomatic communications.

Security Lapses

How good is American security? There's cause for concern, especially after the rash of spies the 1980s disclosed. Over the years, American security has proved to be very poor, much worse than most Americans realize. The case for this conclusion is very clear:

John Walker, in a television interview, stated that "K-Mart has better security than the Navy." This was an authoritative opinion, based upon his tremendously successful experience in his long spying career. He and his confederates were able to walk out of naval installations with cipher keys and other top-secret material without being stopped and searched. Walker was not even caught until several years after he'd retired from the Navy, and then only because his wife snitched to the FBI.

Christopher Boyce, the "Falcon," was able to obtain a top-secret clearance and go to work in one of the most restricted areas in TRW, a top defense contractor, walking out with secrets which his partner, the "Snowman," relayed to the Soviet Embassy in Mexico City. Again, this espionage operation came to light only through a fluke.

Klaus Fuchs, who passed nuclear bomb secrets to the Soviets, was caught only long after he had done so. The FBI learned of him by breaking Soviet codes of the war years. Obviously, his arrest prevented him from passing secrets to the Soviets in the future, but the damage he had already done was significant. The Rosenbergs, also involved in passing nuclear secrets, were able to run their spy ring unmolested by the FBI until a year after the Soviets had detonated their own atom bomb. Conservatively, the Rosenberg Ring was operating for at least ten years.

The top-secret U-2 spy plane was classified, as was almost everything associated with it. There were elaborate schemes to conceal the pilots who flew it, and cover stories to explain its flights, but there was a glaring gap in security. The U-2 jet engine depended upon a small but steady trickle of hydrogen injected into the combustion chamber to prevent "flame-out" at high altitudes. This required carrying a small tank of super-cooled liquid hydrogen aboard the aircraft. Although the movements of the U-2 were classified, liquid hydrogen supplies were not, and this information provided a tip-off to interested parties.[5]

Because espionage is very clandestine, what comes to light is only the tip of the iceberg. The spies who are caught are those who are careless about covering their tracks, those who are very unlucky, and those who operate for so long that the counter-spies eventually discover them.

Part of the reason for our poor success in safeguarding our secrets is that we are an open society. Americans who have never been abroad don't realize how free and open this society is by contrast to those even in Western Europe. In France and Switzerland, for example, it's required to report every change of address to the police. In Soviet Russia, residency permits are required to live in Moscow, and citizens have to comply with a system of internal passports and travel permits. In Britain, the government can prohibit publication of a newspaper or magazine article by administrative fiat. A "D-Notice" to the editor warns him that publication of a certain article, or any information regarding a certain topic, may lead to prosecution under the Official Secrets Act. This effectively stifles publication.

Another aspect is the nature of our security efforts, and the people charged with the responsibility. The armed forces' security services are fairly effective most of the time, but the FBI is seriously deficient because it's still struggling under the Hoover influence.

J. Edgar Hoover had taken over a corrupt and ineffective investigative bureau and professionalized it, but at a price. The FBI's main effort, under Hoover, was seeking personal publicity for the Director. Thus, the FBI had many conspicuous failures. During the 1930s, for example, while Hoover's FBI was building its "gangbusters" image by chasing street thugs, a German spy infiltrated the Norden company and walked away with the design of the Norden Bomb-sight. Hoover's FBI eventually realized the threat, and began working against German agents. The FBI did apprehend many Nazi spies during World War II, while the Soviet networks ran wild through the U.S., stealing nuclear and other military secrets.

Hoover was very turf-conscious, and jealous of what he saw as efforts by other agencies to poach on what he considered "his" territory. A running gun-fight between himself and U.S. Army Intelligence Chief General Sherman Miles came to a head in early 1941. Hoover, who enjoyed a close personal relationship with President Roosevelt, tried to get Miles fired from his post, and only strong efforts by Secretary of the Army Stimson and Chief of Staff George C. Marshall saved Miles' job.[6]

Incidents such as this were common throughout Hoover's career, because they were as symptomatic of Hoover's egotism as they were of Washington political in-fighting. Hoover's Bureau would be involved in squabbles with the OSS during the war, and with its successor agency, the CIA, after the war.

Although Hoover died in 1972, the FBI is still operating according to the same pattern. An important reason for its failures is refusal to accept responsibility for its errors and deficiencies, even in cases which do not have national security aspects. An example is the Miami shoot-out of April 11, 1986, when two street thugs fought eight FBI Agents, killing two and wounding five, before being shot to death themselves. The FBI could not admit that poor training and tactics caused their agents' casualties, instead placing the blame on the handgun ammunition used by the agents.

Unfortunately, these deficiencies are far-reaching. We'll see how they work when we look at the FBI's role in counter-espionage.

Sources

1. *Mask of Treachery*, John Costello, NY, Warner Books, 1988, pp. 431-432.

2. *Territory of Lies*, Wolf Blitzer, NY, Harper Paperbacks, 1989, pp. 287-289.

3. *Spyclopedia*, Richard Deacon, NY, Silver Arrow Books, 1988, p. 337.

4. *Merchants of Treason*, Thomas B. Allen and Norman Polmar, NY, Dell Books, 1988, p. 273.

5. *The Secret Team*, L. Fletcher Prouty, NY, Ballantine Books, 1974, pp. 171-172.

6. *Nazi Spies in America*, William Breuer, NY, St. Martin's Press, 1989, pp. 212-213.

10

Counter-Espionage

The fictional spy faces a court-martial and bravely goes before the firing squad with his mother's name on his lips. At least, that's one romantic image. Reality is different, because in this world of reversed values, the most valuable spy to the target country is one under their control, who feeds false information to his handlers.

Counter-espionage officers appear to get a bum rap in many countries. In the United States, the aristocrats of the Central Intelligence Agency have often looked down upon the FBI, whose agents they considered low-brows. Indeed, for years the typical CIA agent was a graduate of an Ivy League school, while his FBI counterpart graduated from Southern Methodist or Arizona State University. In Britain, the Special Intelligence Service was traditionally the home of the old boys' network, and staffed by graduates of Britain's elite public schools. By contrast, the Security Service, or counter-spies, employed former policemen and the sons of tradesmen. Germany's Gestapo, which was mainly concerned with internal security, was the victim of wartime Allied propaganda which portrayed it as staffed exclusively by sadists. Actually, the Gestapo recruited the cream of German detective forces, and ran the most effective counter-espionage organization in history.

Surveillance

Modern surveillance is both intensive and extensive. It involves traditional shadowing, but also takes in mail and electronic surveillance. Surveillance is both broad-based and includes intensive spot checks on selected individuals.

Broad-based surveillance includes monitoring mail to foreign countries, concentrating on addresses known or suspected of being mail drops for classified information. Counter-espionage agents develop lists of suspicious addresses, based on various criteria. Any foreign address to which government employees send personal mail goes on a provisional list. This is not suspicious in itself, but this may tie in with other information.

Address surveillance led to the discovery of Colonel Alfred Redl's espionage against his native land. Redl, an Austrian officer, had served in the "Kundshafts Stelle," the Austrian counter-espionage service from 1900 to 1911, finishing as its chief. Redl was an innovator, and introduced many new techniques, such as photographing suspects and secretly obtaining their fingerprints. Another technique was the mail watch, and in March, 1913, two envelopes mailed in Eydtkuhnen, in East Prussia, attracted the attention of counter-espionage officers. Eydtkuhnen was known as a center for espionage, because of its proximity to the frontier, and as a convenient place to post mail for espionage purposes. One envelope contained 8,000 crowns, and the other 6,000, but neither contained a covering letter. Both were addressed to Opera Ball 13, General Delivery, Vienna General Post Office.[1]

Counter-espionage officers were intensely interested in the identity of the addressee, and they stationed two detectives to watch the post office. An electrician installed a push-button behind the counter of the general delivery window, to ring a bell in the police station across the street. For some reason now lost to history, both envelopes remained until May 24, when Colonel Redl appeared to pick them up. Detectives followed him, and soon ascertained his identity. When they reported in, word quickly went up to the Chief of the General Staff, who sent a delegation to apprehend Redl. In those days, there was a very strict code of honor, and there was a tacit agreement that Redl would shoot himself. One of the officers left his pistol with him, and the delegation withdrew, leaving Redl to write a short suicide note and dispose of himself.

Upon Redl's death, Austrian counter-espionage officers broke into his apartment in Prague, opened his safe, and examined the contents. The papers they found within told the story. Amazingly, Redl had been betraying his country for over ten years, selling to Russian agents the identities of Austrian agents working in Russia, as well as the army's mobilization and war plan. He had been well-paid for this, allowing him to maintain several residences, including what appeared to be a luxurious love pad in Prague.

The address of any organization known or suspected to be subversive is on a list. This includes both foreign and domestic political organizations, except perhaps the headquarters of the Republican and Democratic parties. Any fringe group, nationalistic organization, racial organization, etc., is on a list. "Front" organizations are on a list. The reason for this is not that members of such organizations are necessarily spies, but are a pool for recruitment by foreign powers.

At times, counter-spies may carry out "black bag jobs," burglaries of suspected premises, to try to obtain information or evidence. A black bag job takes place when the counter-spies either don't want the other side to be aware that they're under intense surveillance, or when there's not enough evidence to authorize a search warrant. Members of MI-5, the British counter-espionage organization, carried out a clandestine search of an apartment rented by a leading member of the Communist Party of Great Britain. This operation, which took place in 1955, resulted in obtaining photocopies of 55,000 files pertaining to members of the party.[2]

Electronic surveillance includes monitoring telephone and telegraph lines, as well as radio bands. Britain's Security Service had been scanning telegrams since the 1920s as a routine measure. For several years, there have been computers which can recognize words and simple phrases, and these can filter through thousands of telephone calls to select those containing suspect words for transcription and study by a human operator.

Radio waves can often carry messages inimical to a country's security, but monitoring these is very difficult. A technological war between illegal transmitters and radio security forces has been going on for decades. During the Second World War, radio sending and detection was mostly manual, with an operator tapping out his message on a telegraph key, and radio direction-finders scanning the horizons for illegal signals. The war did see the first "squirt" radios, however. Today, electronic surveillance is far more difficult, especially in this country, because of the popularity of CB radio and the many unlicensed radios operating on other bands. The sheer volume of "junk" traffic ensures that a spy's transmissions will be lost among the rest, unless he's stupid enough to announce in clear: "Calling Moscow."

It's normal practice to bug the embassies and consulates of foreign powers. An example was Operation "CHOIR," in which MI-5 placed a probe microphone through the wall of the Russian Consulate on Bayswater Road, in London, in 1955. MI-5 also bugged Lancaster House, in London, to eavesdrop on the private conversations of delegates to the Colonial Conferences.

A joint effort between MI-5 and the Royal Canadian Mounted Police resulted in the bugging of the Russian Embassy in Ottawa. These were only a few of the bugging efforts carried out by the British.[3]

Security agents normally watch points of entry, such as airports, seaports, and frontier points. A plainclothes security agent is close by while uniformed customs agents check passports and baggage.

One of the tools of port of entry surveillance is the "watch list," a list of undesirables calling for special treatment. Some are denied entry because of political views or affiliations. One example is Kurt Waldheim, the Austrian statesman and former United Nations Secretary-General. Waldheim is not suspected of being an espionage agent, but is on the American State department list because he was a lieutenant in German army intelligence operating against partisans during World War II. Others are suspected spies, and although agents will allow them into the country, they'll keep a watch on them while they're within the borders. Yet others are in a special category, especially dangerous types who require special handling. A suspected courier may end up with a 24-hour tail while in-country, to observe whom he contacts. Special category types usually have dossiers, and security officers have their faces and descriptions memorized because of their extreme importance.

It's not possible to memorize every person slated for special handling, or even to issue a paper list, because of the tremendous number of names. Frontier control includes watching for drug smuggling, civil criminals, and other categories, as well as security risks. This is why the use of computers has become standard at frontier points. Customs agents punch in passport numbers, license plate numbers, and other identifying data, and alert a security agent if they get a "hit." A hit may be identification of a very dangerous person, or someone using a passport reported lost or stolen.

Specific surveillance can be a routine spot-check, or in response to a lead. A low-priority task for specially-trained surveillance agents is to shadow government employees, selected at random, simply in the hope of uncovering something significant. This also provides a training ground for new agents, scheduled for later assignment to sensitive cases.

Another type of spot-check is intensive random investigation of people with security clearances. This may include a polygraph interrogation, and interrogation with drugs, depending on the method in vogue at the time.

Occasionally, there's an indication of an information leak. This may come from studying an adversary's actions. An increase in overflights of a secret base on foreign shores may show that an agent within the government relayed information about that base. It may also mean that the adversary's coverage on the ground is very effective. Whenever there's evidence that an adversary has information he could not have gotten any other way, there's suspicion of a leak.

Another avenue of information is code-breaking. Deciphering an adversary's secret messages may reveal something he doesn't want us to know, such as his knowledge of something restricted to a small group within the government. Decryption of Soviet traffic led to the uncovering of Klaus Fuchs, the British nuclear scientist.[4]

Leads can also come from defectors. Walter Krivitsky, a general in the Soviet intelligence service, defected to the British in 1937, revealing information they were happy to get. One of the benefits was the identity of a traitor in the code room of the foreign office. Captain John Henry King received a ten-year sentence at his trial in 1939.[5] The notorious Colonel Rudolf Abel was secure in his cover until his aide, Reino Hayhanen, defected and spilled everything to American counter-intelligence.

Hayhanen was a Finn who had risen to the rank of lieutenant-colonel in the KGB. His organization assigned him to be Abel's deputy, sending him to New York. However, the good life corrupted Hayhanen, and Abel viewed his tendency to party and play around with women as neglect of his duties. Hayhanen actually did neglect his job, failing to service dead drops and continuing to operate his transmitter from the same site. Abel got Moscow headquarters to recall Hayhanen, but on the way back, Hayhanen defected to the CIA in Paris. His information led to the arrests of both Abel and U.S. Army Sergeant Roy A. Rhodes, who had passed information to the Russians.[6]

The first step in following up on a lead is to make a list of everyone who had access to the information. If, for example, there's evidence that a foreign country has acquired the technical details of a new torpedo guidance system, the list can be quite long. It will include everyone involved in the system's development, both in the military and civilian industry, including secretaries as well as engineers.

Any specific detail can narrow the focus of the investigation. If it's sure that the foreign espionage service has obtained a certain blueprint, it becomes possible to trace everyone who had access to that blueprint. Modern security practice requires that every copy of every sensitive document be numbered, and that anyone taking or borrowing a copy must sign for it. With a short suspect list, it becomes possible to narrow it further with straight detective work.

A similar situation can arise if a foreign defector brings with him information of a "mole" within the government, or knowledge of top-secret information. He may not know the identity of the mole, but may be able to provide information which limits and focuses the search.

An investigation may begin with a suspicion that an adversary has information he shouldn't, but not progress because the potential suspect list is too large. With the Walker Spy Ring, there was an uncomfortable feeling within the U.S. Navy command that the Soviets simply knew too much about its plans and activities, but the break didn't come until Walker's estranged wife turned him in to the FBI. Even then, the FBI didn't take her information seriously at first.

Some espionage investigations begin with a report from a government or corporate security officer. These are charged with assuring the integrity of security systems, and the human beings who work within them.

Security is a thankless job, and often simply boring. The security officer is often regarded as akin to a keyhole peeper. The best officers don't get assigned to such degrading work, leaving the field to mediocre personalities and intellects. The typical security officer's method of working is uninspiring, prowling offices during the evening to make sure that all safes and drawers containing secret material have been properly shut and locked, and that classified waste paper has gone through the shredder. The security officer's insight into the personalities of people for whom he's responsible is usually very limited, and he typically investigates minor infractions, such as who is sleeping with whom. The security officer also cultivates informers, which does not enhance his popularity.

At times, intensive surveillances begin with the observation of a security officer that one of his charges is behaving out of pattern. Both government and corporate security officers have the opportunity to get to know some of the people they monitor, and they may notice the lowly-paid clerk who buys an expensive car or watch. This inevitably leads to questions regarding the source of his new-found affluence. At times, a fellow employee may report a suspicious person for heavy drinking, or other drastic change in behavior. Emotional mood swings can also signal a drastic change in lifestyle.

The problem with such signals is that they're ambiguous. A fellow employee's report may be sincere, but inaccurate. It may also be the result of personal jealousy, or office politics. When it's possible to denounce a detested rival to the company secret policeman without fear of reprisal, the temptation to cause trouble is too strong for some to resist. Another possibility is that there is an innocent explanation for the signal. Sudden affluence can result from an inheritance, or a lucky hit in the stock market. Depression and drinking can be the result of a failing marriage, or the death of a friend or relative. The security officer who tries to run down every potential lead will soon acquire the reputation of "snooper," and the fallout from this, with the erosion of confidence, can outweigh the advantages. The Big Brother atmosphere can be oppressive, and employees may simply decide that it's better not to speak to the security officer unless he speaks first.

Some security officers revel in unpopularity, maintaining that resentment from the people whom they oversee is proof that they're doing their jobs properly. Major "Sammy" Sansom, who was security officer at the British embassy in Cairo during the late 1940s, appeared proud of being a hard-nose. He ferreted out examples of misbehavior which offended his code of morality, and in the process had several embassy secretaries sent home for having affairs with the local color. He also reported Donald Maclean for his rampant alcoholism, but appears to have totally missed Maclean's spying for the Soviets.[7]

Sometimes, the signals are so blatant that there's no excuse for ignoring them. Jerry Whitworth, a major participant in the Walker Spy Ring, lived a very opulent lifestyle for someone earning a Navy petty officer's pay. He rented a Rolls-Royce, spent a weekend in San Francisco doing the town with his wife, and bought more cars and appliances than his pay would allow.[8] Somehow, Whitworth's shipmates and superior officers overlooked the incongruity of a petty officer spending $726 on hotel accommodations for himself and his wife, the $500 box seats at the opera, and various art treasures he bought both for decorations and as investments. In 1983, Mr. and Mrs. Whitworth had spent about $130,000, although Whitworth's pay was about $23,000.

In certain instances, counter-spies have information handed to them on a platter and ignore it, as in the case of the Walker Spy Ring. John Walker's ex-wife, Barbara, telephoned the FBI office in Hyannis Port, Massachusetts, on November 17, 1984, to reveal that she was willing to tell all about her ex-husband's activities. A few days later, she met an FBI agent and told him the details. The FBI simply dropped the ball, and did not pursue the matter at the time, perhaps because they had heard similar stories from too many spiteful ex-wives.[9]

This was not the first time that the FBI had stubbed its toe. In 1941, the British sent one of their best double agents to the United States to bring the FBI into the picture. He had with him a questionnaire given to him by his German spymasters, but the FBI did not draw the correct conclusions. Many of the questions related to the defenses at Pearl Harbor, as the Germans were trying to help with a Japanese request. Hoover and his agents, however, were put off by the British agent's opulent, luxurious lifestyle, and failed to attach enough importance to the documents he gave them.[10] The FBI's repressive morality was such that one agent confronted the visitor on a beach and threatened to arrest him for violation of the Mann Act.

An unequivocal lead comes when a loyal citizen reports an approach by a spy recruiter. Counter-spies then work the case with three goals. The first is to safeguard their nation's secrets. They carefully control the information the citizen passes to his control officer, to prevent very delicate information from disclosure. They may also try to pass false information, to mislead the enemy agency.

The second purpose is to discover the extent of the network, and find out for whom the control agent is working, and the identities of others he may be running. Agents keep a close watch on the control, following him home or to his office, and noting everyone else he contacts. This is far more important than scooping him up for a quick trial. It's better to have 100 spies under observation, than to imprison one and have 99 running loose.

The third purpose is gathering evidence for prosecution. This is usually the easiest part, given the circumstances. The cooperative citizen hands over a package of secret information at a pre-arranged time and place, and watching government agents swoop in to arrest the contact.

Damage Control

The big question facing a government whose security agents have just unmasked a spy is "How much has he hurt us?" Finding the answer to that question is called "damage control."

This is a thorough investigative process, checking documents and interviewing all of the spy's associates, to identify what information he had within reach, and which he might have turned over to his control. The reason this has to be a careful and slow process is that a spy often has access to far more information than his nominal job description might suggest. Even highly classified documents are often not under tight enough control, as the Pollard case proved.

A defector from a government security agency can provide not only the information derived from his specific duties, but the names of many people who interviewed him, trained him, and served with him. He can bring with him office gossip, details about other employees' personal lives, and other useful information.

Tracing The Network

It's axiomatic that a spy doesn't usually operate alone. He has a control officer, and perhaps a courier or two, to support him. Because it's necessary to maintain a spy, and to collect information from him, this network of contacts becomes a target for the counter-spy. This is why immediately arresting a spy is a poor tactic, just as it is when a loyal citizen informs the counter-espionage agency that a foreign agent is trying to recruit him.

It's better to restrict his access to information, while placing him under intensive round-the-clock surveillance. This can disclose his methods of communication, and lead counter-spies to his contacts. Spotting the spy's handler provides unequivocal indication of who the spy's employer really is. Arresting the spy and asking him the identity of his employer may not be productive, because he may not know. As we've seen, some spies work for people whom they believe represent one country, but in reality the information they deliver goes to another. Another benefit is that a handler may easily have several spies working for him, and shadowing him can reveal these.

Double Cross

One of the important decisions upon arresting a spy is whether to punish or "turn" him. Arrest, trial, and sentencing satisfy the interests of justice, and are often excellent propaganda to show citizens that the security forces are doing their job. There's also good propaganda value in showing how a foreign power is inimical enough to recruit spies to work against the host government.

The alternative is to keep the apprehension secret, and to engage the captured agent against his former employer. This requires the active cooperation of the agent, and he has to make his decision quickly, before anyone notices his absence. The price of his life is betraying his former employer and comrades.

One of the most successful of these operations was the large and long-lasting "double-cross" system used by British counter-spies against the Germans during World War II. This began with a simple "turning" operation before the war by the Security Service's Section B1A, and grew to encompass all German agents in Britain. The system worked to control the enemy espionage networks, catch new agents as they arrived, disclose information about the methods of the German espionage service, reveal code and cipher systems, allow inferences regarding German plans based on the information agents sought, affect German plans by deceptive information, and to fool the enemy about British plans.[11]

It would be a mistake to ascribe the success of the "double-cross" system solely to British cleverness and mastery of the spygame. As we'll see, many agents the Germans recruited, especially after the outbreak of war, were low-grade and poorly-motivated. The German spy chief, Admiral Canaris, depended on quantity, not quality.

Pro-active Measures

Counter-espionage work is essentially police work, and its biggest weakness is that it's often simply reactive. The counter-espionage agent enters the picture after the damage is done, much like the police officer who shows up at a crime scene to take a report. When top officials of a government agency find that its secrets are leaking, they yell for the counter-spies, although they may have declined to follow basic security measures before the incident. However, because they operate in secret, counter-spies have more latitude to use "pro-active" means to combat espionage.

A favorite tactic with counter-espionage agencies is "coat-trailing." A person may walk into a foreign embassy with what appears to be interesting documents for sale. Another type is the set-up, the person with access to secrets who behaves as a conspicuous security risk. He may drink too heavily, cheat on his wife, or even behave as a sexual deviate, to catch the attention of foreign talent-spotters.

The FBI has a record of dangling attractive scams before foreign intelligence agents. At times, they organize walk-ins. A more subtle way is to have a tempting contact show himself, and let the Soviets try to recruit him. One such was an engineer for Grumman Aviation, who was a double agent for the FBI. He passed classified material to Valery Markelov, who nominally worked as a translator at the United Nations in New York. Markelov did not have diplomatic immunity, and he was arrested for trying to steal classified information regarding the F-14 Tomcat Navy fighter.[12]

Another was Lieutenant Commander Arthur Lindstrom, a naval officer near retirement, who took a week-long cruise on a Soviet cruise ship in 1977. The expectation was that a crew member working for Soviet Intelligence would approach him, but none did. Lindstrom was apparently prepared for this, because on leaving the ship, he handed a note to one of the ship's officers, disclosing his availability for recruitment and giving a pay phone number in New Jersey. A Soviet spyhandler contacted him, and Lindstrom passed on information which counter-spies checked to ensure that it wasn't too revealing. This led to the arrest of three Soviets, only one of whom had diplomatic immunity.[13]

Once a foreign agent makes an approach, the counter-spies have several choices. If all they need is a quick and dirty success, they can have the coat-trailer pass secret documents and arrest the recipient. This can result in a show trial, strictly for propaganda. Another technique is to use this conduit to feed false information to the foreign spymaster. The information may be unremarkable, or it may be part of a larger plan to induce the rival power to waste resources. Falsified documents relating to a new weapon system can persuade the foreign government to spend many man-hours devising counter-measures.

The best way to run such an operation is not to fabricate the weapon system out of thin air, because this is simply too hard to do. Instead, it's easier, and more credible, to falsify documents relating to the performance of an unsuccessful design. The enemy will be aware, for example, that a new jet fighter is under development. If the design appears to be unpromising, leaking information that it's a superior performer can induce an enemy to copy its design in his new development program, until he finds out for himself that its shortcomings outweigh its virtues.

Yet another way to profit from a coat-trailer is to run a double agent, one who tries to penetrate the foreign espionage organization while reporting back to the counter-spies. This tactic is unlikely to be very successful, because spymasters feel that anyone who has betrayed his employer is too untrustworthy to accept fully. Still, the penetration agent can set up his foreign contacts for observation and surveillance, with meets covered by surveillance experts. Shadowing his contacts can lead to other members of the foreign espionage ring, and to safe-houses and mail drops. If the coat-trailer has a long career, he may well help uncover a series of contacts, because couriers, control agents, and even residents are rotated periodically. Every several years the coat-trailer will find his control handing him over to a new control agent.

Another pro-active measure is to set up a totally fake secret organization as a lure. One of the most successful such operations was "The Trust," set up by Felix Dzerzhinsky, who was the first chief of the CHEKA. The Trust was ostensibly an anti-communist organization within Russia, set up by two CHEKA agents, Yakushev and Opperput. This tactic lured counter-revolutionaries back to the motherland, where the CHEKA could arrest and dispose of them.

The CHEKA became the OGPU in 1923. One of the spectacular victims of "The Trust" was Boris Savinkov, a noted leader of the anti-Bolsheviks, who while in OGPU hands died in a fall from a window in 1925. The death was supposedly suicide, but defenestration is one of the ways the Soviet secret police use to dispose of awkward people. Jan Masaryk, the Czech patriot, also went out of a window in Czechoslovakia in 1948 while under the control of the KGB.[14]

An extraordinarily successful pro-active operation climaxed in the "Venlo Incident," during which two British spymasters fell into the hands of the German Sicherheitsdienst. The British SIS had set up two parallel intelligence services on the continent of Europe before World War II. When the war broke out, London ordered the two control officers, S. Payne Best and Richard Stevens, to merge their organizations for efficiency. Best and Stevens had their headquarters in The Hague, in neutral Holland. Apparently Colonel Claude Dansey, in overall charge from London, thought that the Germans would behave as during the last war, and not overrun Holland. However, Best and Stevens were to become captives before the country came under occupation.

Walter Schellenberg, one of the SD's rising stars, posed as "Captain Schaemmel," a supposed member of a group of dissident officers in the Wehrmacht. He led Best and Stevens through negotiations which were to lead to Hitler's overthrow and a peace settlement, to lure them within reach of a kidnap team. On November 9, 1939, Best and Stevens drove to Venlo, a Dutch border town, to meet with the plot's leader, a general. A team of SS commandos, in a large open car, crashed through the border gate and pulled up next to Best and Stevens in the parking lot of the cafe where the meeting was to take place. This was only a few yards across the frontier. There was a short exchange of gunfire, killing Lieutenant Klop, the Dutch liaison officer. SS troopers bundled Best and Stevens into the car, which then drove backwards into German territory.[15]

Russian and German "stings" were very successful. The problem that arose with the FBI's coat-trailing operations was that the FBI appeared to concentrate on the quick and easy victories brought by these "stings." Instead of undertaking the laborious and difficult work of ferreting out genuine American traitors and uncovering infiltrators, the FBI set up Soviet officers for quick arrests and show trials.[16]

This helps build up a public perception that the FBI is on the job, and that the country's security is in good hands, but it's only show. Behind the scenes, foreign spies continue unmolested, and with the greatest incentive not to expose the FBI's weakness.

Sometimes, however, a genuine spy gets caught. As we'll see, the spy caught in the United States has an even chance of an exchange, or parole. Spies caught in other countries, however, often don't get such lenient treatment.

Sources

1. *Cry Spy*, Burke Wilkinson, Englewood Cliffs, NJ, Bradbury Press, 1969, pp. 4-12.

2. *Spycatcher*, Peter Wright, NY, Dell Books, 1987, pp. 68-69.

3. *Ibid.*, pp. 69-81.

4. *The FBI-KGB War*, Robert J. Lamphere, NY, Berkeley Books, 1987, pp. 137-140.

5. *Ibid.*, p. 245.

6. *Spyclopedia*, Richard Deacon, NY, Silver Arrow Books, 1988, pp. 308-309.

7. *Catching Spies*, H.H.A. Cooper and Lawrence J. Redlinger, NY, Bantam Books, 1990, pp. 168-169.

8. *Merchants of Treason*, Thomas B. Allen and Norman Polmar, NY, Dell Books, 1988, pp. 121-126.

9. *Ibid.*, p. 293.

10. *The Double-Cross System*, J. C. Masterman, NY, Avon, 1972, pp. 122-124.

11. *Ibid.*, pp. 95-96.

12. *Merchants of Treason*, p. 202.

13. *Ibid.*, pp. 206-207.

14. *Spyclopedia*, pp. 251-252.

15. *Ibid.*, pp. 255-256.

16. *Merchants of Treason*, p. 202.

11

The Spy Who Gets Caught

〰〰〰〰〰〰〰〰〰〰〰〰〰〰〰〰〰〰〰〰〰〰〰〰〰〰〰〰〰

Inevitably, some spies are caught by counter-espionage forces. Every spymaster knows this, and develops a certain cynicism regarding his agents' prospects of evading detection.

The chances of getting caught depend on several factors. An important one is the training and preparation given the agent. If you're working for your country as an infiltration agent, and you get a couple of years' training, a good set of documents, and tangible help inside the target country, you may be able to operate unmolested for years. If your assignment is to be a "sleeper," you'll be left alone to establish yourself and perfect your cover before you have to go to work. You can take comfort that the odds are in your favor.

If, on the other hand, you get a few weeks' hurried training, and end up at the end of a parachute one dark night, dropping into unknown territory, your chances of survival are poor, no matter what your spymaster boss may have told you. The hurried training and incomplete preparations are typical of wartime expediency, when numbers count more than quality.

Before and during World War II, Germany's Admiral Canaris was in charge of the "Abwehr," the army's foreign espionage service. Canaris was under pressure of time, and had to produce quick results. Therefore, he used large numbers of hastily-prepared agents, sending them into Britain and the United States via parachute, submarine, and any other means available, in the hope that some would survive long enough to accomplish their missions.[1]

This was in sharp contrast to the tactics of his predecessor in the Abwehr, Colonel Fritz Gempp, who worked during the 1920s to plant agents in the United States. Gempp sent his first agent over in 1927, and because at the time there were no prospects of immediate war, Gempp was able to take his time and do the job right. Each agent he sent was well-prepared, and indeed, none were caught until after Canaris had become Abwehr chief. Gempp's ace agent was almost caught, after Canaris had taken over the helm, but managed to talk his way free after a customs agent had discovered secret papers in his violin case in New York.[2]

The spy caught in the act faces a gloomy future with few choices. He can confess and cooperate to save his life, betraying his associates and his handler. He can "tough it out," against impossible odds, and face the firing squad or a long prison term. He can also hope for an exchange, which is a real prospect between countries not at war.

Typically, his instructions will be to stall upon capture, and to stonewall his interrogators at all costs, for a few hours to a few days. This is to allow the handler, couriers, and other accomplices to flee to safety.

Cover Stories

Publicly, the government for which he is working will disavow or discredit him. The cover story may be that he is a businessman framed for espionage by a dictatorial government, etc. The cover story usually has several parts, each designed for a different contingency. Getting through the cover story is like peeling an onion, with layer after layer discarded, leaving one wondering if the latest is the final and true version.

The first version is total denial, and ignorance of the alleged spy: "We never heard of him."

If the spy turns out to be a citizen of the nation accused of masterminding him, the cover story changes to accommodate this: "He is a citizen, but he's not working for the intelligence service, and he's totally innocent of any espionage."

If the captor presents evidence that the alleged spy did penetrate a security zone, as happened with aircraft at various times, the cover story now changes to state that the penetration was accidental or inadvertent: "The pilot got lost in bad weather." Another variant is: "He took a streetcar for the zoo, and got off at the wrong stop."

If the captor presents evidence of espionage, such as possession of classified documents, the cover story now may become: "He was framed. Their security agents planted the papers on him just to embarrass us."

If the spy confesses, a common cover story is that the confession was coerced: "They beat it out of him."

If the spy shows no signs of beatings or other abuse during a public trial, or upon exhibition to the international press, the cover story changes once more, to claim that psychological methods were used: "He was brainwashed. They used powerful drugs to mess with his mind."

If, as in both the U-2 and Pollard Affairs, there are confessions and physical evidence to leave no doubt about the truth of the charges, there's yet another story. Deniability is important, to protect the head of government. The accused government admits the act, but claims that it was an unauthorized operation: "The Colonel did it all by himself, without telling his superiors. He was a rogue, a wild card." The Israeli government used this story in explaining espionage upon an ally, when American counter-spies caught Jonathan Pollard passing secret documents, placing the blame on an Israeli Air Force colonel. This was also the story when the Israeli government got caught sabotaging American and British facilities in Egypt, in 1954. The spate of denials laid the blame on Pinhas Lavon, then defense minister, and resulted in a scandal known as the "Lavon Affair."[3]

There are sometimes sacrifices to maintain this cover story. Allen Dulles, Director of Central Intelligence, offered to resign after the U-2 downing, to protect President Eisenhower's image.

The final stage is full admission, but with an imperative justification: "We did the same thing to them that they've been doing to us for years." Another is: "Overriding national security reasons made it important to obtain this information." Yet another is: "We had to know, to maintain peace in the world."

An interesting sidelight of this is the survival instinct of the spy who gets caught. Just as his government often manipulates him, the spy may also manipulate his government when his survival is at stake.

In 1958, when the CIA was trying to overthrow Indonesia's President Sukarno, the agency used "sanitized" B-26 aircraft to provide air support to the rebels. One of these B-26s came to grief while trying to interdict loyalist ships. The pilot, an American named Allen Pope, survived, as did several members of his crew. Pope had with him his U.S. Air Force I.D. cards, and a set of orders that outlined his mission. The reason is that, if Pope had followed orders and carried no I. D. with him, he would have been a non-person, deniable by the U.S. Government, and liable to execution by the Indonesians. As a U.S. pilot, he was a liability to the U.S. Government, and no longer deniable. This gave the Indonesians what they needed to embarrass the United States, and forced the U.S. Government to redeem him, instead of leaving him to his fate.[4]

Obviously, clandestine pilots take steps to circumvent the sanitizing procedures. They may hide I. D. aboard the aircraft, to make sure they have their lifesavers with them despite the precautions their employers impose.

The Fate of the Spy
Who Gets Caught

The spy's fate is hardly ever cut and dried. The noose and firing squad are often merely wartime expedients. It's necessary to have some well-publicized executions during wartime, and even during peacetime, to put stress upon present and future spies and traitors. Sometimes, however, spy trials are secret, and convicted spies and traitors die alone and unknown, their fate kept from publication until after the end of the war.

On June 12, 1942, several German saboteurs came ashore from a U-Boat at Amagansett, Long Island, but had the bad luck to be seen by an American Coast Guardsman. Although they managed to bluff their way out of the immediate area, the Coast Guardsman reported the incident and an intensive search by the FBI began. A second sabotage team landed on the Gulf Coast of Florida, about 25 miles southeast of Jacksonville.

One saboteur, George Dasch, lost his nerve and telephoned the FBI, providing information which led to the round-up of all eight agents within two weeks. At President Roosevelt's direction, the FBI publicized their capture, but their subsequent fate, and the details of the investigation, were deep secrets until after the war. The secret court-martial took place in July, 1942, and six of the eight saboteurs got the death sentence on the morning of August 8, 1942. President Roosevelt approved the sentences, and at about noon the condemned men went to the electric chair.[5]

The current practice of exchanging secret agents makes it all merely a game. An agent who knows that the worst that can happen to him is a few months or years imprisonment before repatriation has less to trouble him than one who knows that a bullet or rope awaits failure. Although in reality, execution isn't a foregone conclusion, the prospect is a deterrent.

Sentences vary, according to the degree of an agent's involvement, and the whim of the court. One example of disparity in sentencing was the treatment of the Israeli espionage/sabotage ring uncovered by Egyptian counter-spies in 1954. In January, 1955, the verdicts came down. There were four death sentences, two of which the Egyptians carried out on the gallows, but two of which were "in absentia," because these two had fled the country. There were two sentences of life imprisonment at hard labor, two of 15 years, one of seven years, one of five years, and two acquittals.[6]

During peacetime, there's much less incentive to put the captured spy to death. There are certain exceptions, however. In some countries, a traitor within the ranks of the intelligence or security services will get the death sentence, after a quick and secret court-martial. This happens when the damage is so great that the department head seeks the harshest reprisal. Although the execution is away from public gaze, the news will be spread throughout the department as a lesson to others.

Another important point is the identity of the spy's employer. The spy who passes secrets to an enemy during wartime is likely to face death, but one who works for an ally has a better chance of escaping with his life. The simple reason for the difference is that information passed to an enemy is more likely to result in the deaths of friendly servicemen.

Special circumstances can also affect the outcome. Much depends upon the degree of his cooperation with his captors. Any security officer working a case wants to extract as much information as he can from a captured spy. The vital details are:

- How long the spy has been working for a foreign power.

- Who recruited him.

- Who trained him.

- How many others in his spy ring.

- Who was his control officer.

- What information was sought by his control.

- What information he actually handed over to his control.

- Means of communication.

- Means of payment.
- Identities of any couriers or others involved in communications.
- Recognition signals and passwords.
- Locations of dead drops, live drops, etc.

Cooperating with captors is one way captured spies buy their lives or their freedom. Jonathan Pollard did not expect to get a life sentence, partly because he'd spied for an ally. The reason he did is that he refused to name other Americans spying for Israel.[7]

Pollard's wife, Anne Henderson-Pollard, went to prison for her role in the affair, but her health quickly declined during confinement, and the government released her in January, 1990, after 40 months. While she was in Mount Sinai Hospital, New York, she received papers relating to a divorce action her husband was filing against her.[8]

Julius and Ethel Rosenberg were part of a larger spy ring than came to light, and FBI Agents were eager to learn the names of others involved. Julius Rosenberg had boasted to his brother-in-law that he actually ran the spy ring.[9] Although his wife's involvement was marginal, government prosecutors charged her with capital espionage to pressure Julius to talk. This was possible because, although Soviet Russia had been our wartime ally when the Rosenbergs passed nuclear data, the anti-communist hysteria of the McCarthy era made severe punishment politically acceptable.

The sentence, death by electrocution, finally took place on June 19, 1953, but the FBI kept an open telephone line to Sing Sing Prison in case one or the other decided to sing. Up to the last minute, the FBI hoped that the threat of death would force the much-needed information from them.[10]

Information made public since the electrocutions has confirmed the suspicion that there were other Soviet spies besides the Rosenbergs operating in the United States at that time. The Rosenberg ring passed design details of the atom bomb, but this was straight-forward engineering, and not the major obstacle to building nuclear weapons. The big problem was obtaining fissile material pure enough for use in nuclear weapons, and the Rosenberg ring did not have access to this information. That the Russians were able to test-fire an atom bomb only four years after the United States had first done it implied that they had the problem of nuclear fuel solved. Peter Kapitza had brought nuclear technology home with him in the 1930s, and the Soviets had been working on it for years. The demands of wartime production made it impossible for the Soviets to make the massive industrial investment a nuclear separation plant required while the war was still going.

Operating nuclear spy rings in the United States, however, gave them access to what we were doing. Given the atmosphere of the time, if the FBI had had any solid leads on other spies, arrests would have shortly followed. We can safely infer that a totally separate Soviet espionage operation was going on at the time, and that the FBI knew nothing about it, either during the war or afterward.

Some spies survive by clever manipulation of their captors. They make it clear that they intend to cooperate, but they don't put all of their cards on the table. They disclose information gradually, doling it out at a measured pace to both ensure their survival and to keep their captors' interest alive. Counter intelligence officers are very eager to obtain even meager scraps of information about the other side, and they easily fall victim to this ploy. The confessing spy's ace in the hole is always to withhold part of the information, so that he can promise more interesting revelations during the next session. Anthony Blunt, the British "Fourth Man," did this very well, and avoided prosecution during his entire life. He also avoided revealing any information with more than historical interest.

This doesn't always work. It's one thing to be facing a gentlemanly British interrogator during peacetime, when breaks for afternoon tea are part of the routine, and work stops for the weekend. A spy uncovered by the Gestapo or SMERSH during wartime faces angry and impatient men, who have no time to waste with people who try to play word games.[11] There is no polite warning that "anything you say may be used against you." Instead, there will be an intense exhortation to tell everything he knows, and possibly a description, in explicit detail, of what will happen to anyone who fails to cooperate.

The recalcitrant spy will find that the gloves come off very quickly, and that broken teeth, kicks to the kidneys, and blows to the groin begin punctuating the interrogators' questions. Immersion in a tub of ice water loosens some tongues, and if a field telephone is available, the interrogating officer will use its magneto to generate a painful, high-voltage current after attaching wires to various sensitive places on the body.

If this doesn't do the trick, there may be one last chance, with the interrogator telling the subject frankly that, if he doesn't show some cooperation, his lights will go out quickly and permanently within the next 24 hours. If time allows, the spy will get a last meal, and a few hours alone to reflect upon whether dying for his cause is worthwhile. At the end, there will be a hurried interview, and if cooperation isn't immediately forthcoming, a quick trip to the firing squad outside.

Graymail

Another trick open to captured spies and traitors is "graymail," the threat to reveal classified or damaging information in court. This may be top-secret information disclosing how counter-intelligence services operate, or the nature of the data they passed to their control agents. The counter-espionage service may not want their country's citizens to learn how successful foreign agents had been in penetrating security. This is especially true because it reflects upon the counter-spies' competence. Graymail allows spies and traitors to cut deals with their captors, and even to work an exchange.

One spy who tried to use graymail was Alfred Frauenknecht, a Swiss citizen who handed over almost the entire set of blueprints of the Swiss-built version of the French Mirage fighter-bomber and its tooling to Israeli agents during 1968 and 1969. At the time, France's President De Gaulle had declared an arms embargo against Israel, and refused to ship either aircraft or spare parts. The Swiss government had adopted the French-designed Mirage for its air force, on the condition that the Swiss firm of Sulzer Brothers construct the planes on Swiss soil. When the Israeli government asked the Swiss government if it would sell them spare parts, the Swiss refused. Their relationship with France, traditionally a friendly neighbor, was too important to risk. Frauenknecht concocted a plan to steal the entire set of blueprints, and sell them to Israeli agents for $200,000.[12]

In September, 1969, during the shipment of the last installment of plans, the plot fell apart. By accident, Swiss counter-intelligence officers learned of the delivery of Mirage blueprints to Israel, and intercepted a portion of the shipment. Upon his arrest, Frauenknecht proposed to his captors that, if released, he would keep the affair quiet. He pointed out that public disclosure of how Swiss authorities had been so lax as to allow the Mirage plans to be stolen would sour relations between the two governments. The Swiss prosecutor wasn't buying, however, and Frauenknecht had to stand trial for his acts.

Graymail can only work in an open society, however, as totalitarian ones are not vulnerable to this. In a closed society, the counter-espionage service can hold a prisoner incommunicado, arrange a secret trial, and a quick execution. This is the "administrative disposition" of a case.

Turning Spies

Although shooting or hanging a spy or traitor provides short-term satisfaction, in the long run it may be more beneficial to let a captured spy live, if it's possible to use him against his foreign employer. A captured spy who cooperates fully can be very valuable in several ways; he can:

- Feed false information to his control officer.

- Continue to absorb resources of the enemy espionage service.

- Lead counter-spies to his control officer, couriers, or even other agents.

- Lure additional agents into range, for capture by counter-spies.

During World War II, British counter-spies ran a comprehensive and sophisticated operation to fool the Germans into thinking that they had a complete espionage network operating in Britain. Actually, as British counter-spies gradually realized, every German agent in Britain was operating under British control. This was the famous "Double-cross" system, which the British used to fake out German spymasters, and to pass disinformation about the Normandy Invasion.

On the German side, one of the ace Abwehr investigators, Major Hermann Giskes, ran "Operation North Pole," which dismantled the British Special Operations Executive network in Holland and lured many agents into captivity. In 1941, the British parachuted a radio operator, Hubert Lauwers, into Holland, where the Abwehr captured him. Under pressure from his interrogators, Lauwers agreed to transmit messages dictated by the Germans. In so doing, he omitted his "security check," a code word or phrase to indicate that he was not under duress. He also managed to insert the word "caught" in several places, but British operators ignored this. Major Giskes built this first success into an entire imaginary network, luring about 100 British agents into Holland, and capturing tons of air-dropped supplies.[13]

Exchanging Spies

During peacetime, opposing countries sometimes exchange spies. One noted example was the exchange of Colonel Rudolf Ivanovich Abel for Francis Gary Powers, the U-2 pilot. Abel was a Soviet resident who had been running spies from Brooklyn, New York, while posing as a photographer. Spy swaps are not new, nor are they a manifestation of a declining cold war. Maxim Litvinov, a Russian spy who later became Soviet Foreign Minister and Ambassador to the United States, was the beneficiary of a deal between the British government and the new Soviet regime after his arrest in 1918. The Soviets had arrested Robert Bruce Lockhart, sent by the Secret Intelligence Service to foment overthrow of the Bolsheviks. The two governments cut a deal and exchanged agents.[14] Another exchange, this time between Soviet Russia and the United States, took place in 1941. Gaik Ovakimian, a Soviet resident in this country since 1933, was arrested by the FBI in May, 1941. The State Department arranged for his exchange for several Americans held in Russia, in July, 1941, and Ovakimian was home free.[15]

Exchanges are not necessarily for spies and agents of equal value. By contrast with Abel, the master spy, Powers was just a bus driver.

Selecting those for exchange has its own rationale. One country may be very happy to give up a low-level agent to recover one of their important ones. It may also be expedient to hand over a super-star for a relatively obscure agent, to avoid a public trial which would reveal how much that spy had stolen before being caught. A trial would only raise embarrassing questions about the counter-espionage agency's competence.

Arrests of spies tend to go in pairs, with an arrest on one side quickly followed by an arrest on the other side. When the FBI arrested three Soviet agents in the Lindstrom sting operation, the Soviets began organizing a matching operation. Only one of the Soviets had diplomatic immunity, and he quickly was released and left the country. The other two had to face charges. Two months after the arrests, the KGB arrested F. Jay Crawford, an American tractor company manager in Moscow on a charge of smuggling. A rather convoluted exchange took place, with the two Soviets on one side being traded for the freedom of five Soviet dissidents, Crawford, and some additional concessions which remain secret.[16]

There is also the frame, the citizen of the other country entrapped, or burdened with planted evidence, to generate a person for exchange. All governments deny framing anyone, stating that this dirty trick is the exclusive business of the rival power, but they can't all be right. There were assertions that Crawford, the American arrested on smuggling charges in Moscow, had been the victim of a KGB frame to generate a body for exchange.

Setting up a frame can be extremely simple. One alleged frame was that of Nicholas Daniloff, an employee of *U.S. News & World Report*, in Moscow. One of Daniloff's Soviet acquaintances handed him an envelope, and the KGB stepped in for the arrest. The envelope contained documents of military value, according to the KGB, and they held Daniloff as a spy.[17]

Sources

1. *Nazi Spies in America*, William Breuer, NY, St. Martin's Press, 1989, pp. 117-118.

2. *Ibid.*, pp. 24-30.

3. *Decline of Honor*, Avri El-Ad, Chicago, Henry Regnery Company, 1976, pp. 178-219.

4. *The Secret Team*, L. Fletcher Prouty, NY, Ballantine Books, 1974, pp. 362-366.

5. *Nazi Spies in America*, pp. 278-283.

6. *Decline of Honor*, p. 211.

7. *Territory of Lies*, Wolf Blitzer, NY, Harper Paperbacks, 1989, p. 299.

8. Mesa, Arizona, *Tribune,* July 20, 1990.

9. *The FBI-KGB War,* Robert J. Lamphere, NY, Berkeley Books, 1987, p. 192.

10. *Ibid.,* p. 278.

11. *Catching Spies,* H.H.A. Cooper and Lawrence J. Redlinger, NY, Bantam Books, 1990, p. 15.

12. *The Mossad,* Dennis Eisenberg, Uri Dan, and Eli Landau, NY, Paddington Press, 1978, pp. 211-227.

13. *Spyclopedia,* Richard Deacon, NY, Silver Arrow Books, 1988, pp. 225-226.

14. *Merchants of Treason,* Thomas B. Allen and Norman Polmar, NY, Dell Books, 1988, p. 38.

15. *The FBI-KGB War,* p. 25.

16. *Merchants of Treason,* pp. 206-211.

17. *Ibid.,* p. 215.

Glossary

Agent One operating as a spy, traitor, or handler. Exact definition depends upon context. A "penetration agent" worms his way into the other side's establishment, although his career is not as long as a mole's.

Agent of Influence One who is in a position to affect policy and/or opinion in the target country. This is his main function, and he generally does not gather information.

Agent Provocateur An agent used for entrapment. A decoy. The provocateur may be a false defector or walk-in, to entrap a diplomat into a compromising position.

Background Check Investigation of a subject's history, as a prelude to hiring, or as a periodic review of his security clearance.

Barium Meal A piece of information fed to a suspected spy or traitor that is so important that he'll feel compelled to pass it along immediately. This provides the opportunity for counter-spies to shadow him to his contact, or to watch for any signs that the information is in the hands of the other side.

Black Bag Job An illegal break-in, by security police acting without a warrant.

Blow To disclose or expose a clandestine agent or operation.

Brush Contact A seemingly casual brushing by another person while walking, to quickly and clandestinely exchange material.

Burn Extremely damaging disclosure of an agent or operation, so severe that it ends its usefulness.

Case Officer American term for "control officer" or "handler."

Coat-trailing Setting up a decoy operation to uncover a control agent or to feed false information to a foreign power.

Control, Control Agent The agent who gives the spy his orders, pays him, and who receives his material. The control agent may not meet face-to-face with his spy or traitor, but may use cut-outs or dead drops. See "handler," and "case officer."

Counter-spy A security agent specializing in working espionage cases, rather than enforcing routine security.

Courier A messenger, used to transmit messages, money, and other material between members of a spy ring. The courier may have special privileges, enabling him to travel freely, or another advantage that minimizes the risk of discovery.

Cut-out A courier used to break the trail between one agent and another. The courier's sole function is to ensure that an agent does not come face to face with his controller or with other agents.

Dead Drop A place to deposit material for later pickup by another.

Defector One who goes over to the other side. This is another word for "traitor."

Defector-in-place One who changes loyalties, but does not physically go over to the other side. Instead, he remains within the country, at his job, and passes sensitive information to his handler. He may eventually go over, after his usefulness is over, or when it appears that discovery is imminent.

Dirty Tricks A repertoire of illegal activities, such as break-ins, assassination, blackmail, etc., usually assigned to a special group within an espionage organization.

Disinformation An operation undertaken to mislead an enemy or rival, often using faked information or documents.

Dubok Russian term for dead drop.

False Flag A technique in which the control agent adopts another nationality, to persuade the recruit to work for him. False flag recruiting is sometimes necessary because the recruit would object to working for the control agent's real employer.

Flutter CIA slang for polygraph examination.

Front A social or political organization, set up to provide a cover for an illicit or hidden purpose.

Graymail A captured spy's manipulation of his captors by threatening to reveal secret or embarrassing information during his trial.

GRU Soviet Military Intelligence.

Handler The person in charge of an agent or spy. He does not do any spying himself, but remains in the background, to receive transmitted material and to pay the agent. See "Control."

Honey-pot Sexual enticement often used to recruit or blackmail agents.

Illegal An agent who has entered the country on false papers.

KGB Acronym for the Soviet security and intelligence service, which has also had other names in the past, such as CHEKA, OGPU, GPU, NKVD, MVD, MGB, and MOOP. Not to be confused with GRU, Soviet Military Intelligence.

L-Pill A poison pill, for use if captured, to prevent suffering from torture, and the risk of revealing damaging information.

Legal Agent One who is in the target country as an accredited representative of his country, often under diplomatic immunity.

Live Drop A meeting to pass or exchange material between two members of an espionage organization.

Mail Drop An address for sending material. Preferably one which arouses no suspicion and which is not under surveillance.

Mokrie Dela Russian for "wet affairs," or "wet work," slang for the dirty tricks department. Also known as the "Department of Dirty Water." The British "Special Operations Executive," during World War II was such an organization. Some of its actions were so dirty that the British Government ordered its records burned at the end of the war.

Mole An agent deep inside the government, passing information while remaining undiscovered for years.

Need-to-know Compartmenting of information, to restrict knowledge to those who must have it to do their jobs.

Persona A character or identity built up to serve a special purpose.

PNG Persona Non Grata, a diplomatic term for a guest no longer welcome. A diplomat, caught in unseemly behavior, may get "PNGed," and be told to leave forthwith. The term is pronounced "pinged."

Resident Master spy, or control agent, in charge of one or more agents in a particular country. He is called the "resident" because he usually lives there. There are exceptions, though, because it's more secure to run an operation from a neighboring country, especially if the resident does not have diplomatic immunity.

Sabotage Destruction of a target country's economic or military resources. Sabotage isn't necessarily restricted to wartime, but can occur during peacetime as a means of gaining an advantage over a rival or potential enemy without war. At times, espionage agents carry out sabotage missions.

Safe House A refuge, usually a house or apartment where an agent can hide during an emergency. To be secure, a safe house must be totally unknown and unsuspected by counter-spies.

Sanitize To remove all identification documents, labels, and marks. A sanitized agent must go into a room where he strips down, leaving everything behind him as he goes into the next room to dress in untraceable clothing. Aircraft and ships are also sanitized, all serial numbers and identifying marks removed, to obscure the country of origin. This doesn't work as well with ships and planes, because designs give the game away. However, a plane can be built from spare parts, covering its previous owner or purchaser.

Security Check A code word or phrase in a radio message, to indicate that the operator is not transmitting under duress. This can be a word, number, or a purposeful misspelling of a certain word.

Security Clearance Permission by security authorities, after an investigation, to hold a sensitive position.

Security Service Government police agency directed at countering espionage. The American FBI handles security duties, as does the British DI-5 and the Soviet KGB.

Service To visit regularly, and to attend to needs. An agent "services" a dead drop, for example, by regular visits to pick up any messages.

Sleeper An agent who does nothing after establishing himself in place, and awaits an activation order from his handler.

Squirt Radio A radio with a two-speed tape recorder built in. You record your message at normal speed before transmission. When you make contact with your base station, you push a button and the tape plays back at high speed, transmitting the entire message in a "burst" of just a few seconds. This reduces your time on the air, supposedly not allowing the enemy direction-finders time to get a fix on your location.

Turning Inducing a captured agent to work for you against his original employer.

Index

YOU WILL ALSO WANT TO READ:

☐ **55082 A PRACTICAL GUIDE TO PHOTOGRAPHIC INTELLI-GENCE,** *by Harold Hough.* A guide to taking and interpreting surveillance photographs. Learn how to: Take useful photos of objects miles away, and determine their dimensions • Read documents burned to an ash • Take aerial photographs • Use infrared light to capture invisible images • Develop film anywhere, anytime • And much more. Includes actual spy photographs and many helpful illustrations. *1990, 5½ x 8½, 136 pp, illustrated, soft cover.* **$16.95.**

☐ **55072 THE MUCKRAKERS MANUAL, How to Do Your Own In-vestigative Reporting** *by M Harry.* How to dig out the dirt onanyone! Written for investigative reporters exposing political corruption, the detailed professional investigative techniques are useful to any investigation. Developing "inside" sources • Getting documents • Incredible ruses that really work • Interviewing techniques • Infiltration • When to stop an investigation • Protecting your sources • And much more, including an extensive bibliography. *1984, 5½ x 8½, 148 pp, illustrated, soft cover.* **$12.95.**

☐ **55052 SHADOWING & SURVEILLANCE,** *by Burt Rapp.* This is a no-nonsense guide to shadowing and surveillance techniques with an emphasis on do-it-yourself, low-support methods. Tailing on foot and in a car • How to lose a tail • Using decoys and disguises • Searching property • Photographic surveillance tech-niques • How to conduct a stakeout • Electronic surveillance • And much more. *1986, 5½ x 8½, 136 pp, illustrated, soft cover.* **$14.95**

☐ **55053 UNDERCOVER WORK,** *by Burt Rapp.* Undercover operations have acquired a mystique and image of glamour that overshadows how truly grimy they usually are. This book gives the real inside story on how undercover operations are conducted. Contents include: • Getting Started • Training Agents • Establishing Cover • Infiltration • Gaining Confidence • Using Informers • Blackmail • Entrap-ment • Industrial Espionage • Planting Evidence • Getting Paid • And Much More. *1986, 5½ x 8½, 143 pp, soft cover.* **$12.95.**

And much more! We offer the very finest in controversial and unusual books — please turn to our catalog announcement on the next page.

ESP91

LOOMPANICS UNLIMITED
PO Box 1197
Port Townsend, WA 98368

Please send me the titles I have checked above. I have enclosed $ _____ (including $3.00 for shipping and handling for 1 to 3 books, $6.00 for 4 or more.).

Name _____

Address _____

City/State/Zip _____

(Washington residents include 7.8% sales tax.)

"Yes, there are books about the skills of apocalypse — spying, surveillance, fraud, wiretapping, smuggling, self-defense, lockpicking, gunmanship, eavesdropping, car chasing, civil warfare, surviving jail, and dropping out of sight. Apparently writing books is the way mercenaries bring in spare cash between wars. The books are useful, and it's good the information is freely available (and they definitely inspire interesting dreams), but their advice should be taken with a salt shaker or two and all your wits. A few of these volumes are truly scary. Loompanics is the best of the Libertarian suppliers who carry them. Though full of 'you'll-wish-you'd-read-these-when-it's-too-late' rhetoric, their catalog is genuinely informative."

—**THE NEXT WHOLE EARTH CATALOG**

THE BEST BOOK CATALOG IN THE WORLD!!!

We offer hard-to-find books on the world's most unusual subjects. Here are a few of the topics covered IN DEPTH in our exciting new catalog:

- *Hiding/concealment of physical objects! A complete section of the best books ever written on hiding things!*

- *Fake ID/Alternate Identities! The most comprehensive selection of books on this little-known subject ever offered for sale! You have to see it to believe it!*

- *Investigative/Undercover methods and techniques! Professional secrets known only to a few, now revealed to you to use! Actual police manuals on shadowing and surveillance!*

- *And much, much more, including Locks and Locksmithing, Self-Defense, Intelligence Increase, Life Extension, Money-Making Opportunities, and more!*

Our book catalog is 8½ x 11, packed with over 500 of the most controversial and unusual books ever printed! You can order every book listed! Periodic supplements to keep you posted on the LATEST titles available!!! Our catalog is free with the order of any book on the previous page — or is $5.00 if ordered by itself.

Our book catalog is truly THE BEST BOOK CATALOG IN THE WORLD! Order yours today — you will be very pleased, we know.

LOOMPANICS UNLIMITED
PO BOX 1197
PORT TOWNSEND, WA 98368
USA